Theft

A play

Eric Chappell

Samuel French — London
New York - Toronto - Hollywood

Printed at Redwood Books, Trowbridge, Wiltshire.

THEFT

First presented at the Theatre Royal, Windsor, on 28th
June 1995, with the following cast:

Trevor Farrington	David Simeon
John Miles	Terence Booth
Jenny Farrington	Sue Holderness
Barbara Miles	Penny Morrell
Spriggs	George Cole

Directed by Mark Piper
Designed by Alexander McPherson
Lighting by Mark Doubleday

CHARACTERS

Trevor Farrington, late 40s
John Miles, late 40s
Jenny Farrington, younger than Trevor
Barbara Miles, older than Jenny
Spriggs, 50s

The action takes place in John and Barbara Miles' house
in the country

SYNOPSIS OF SCENES

ACT I

ACT II

Time — the present

ACT I

SCENE 1

The large drawing-room of the country house owned by John and Barbara Miles. Night

The room has been comfortably and expensively furnished. US *is an Adam fireplace either side of which are bookcases filled with leatherbound volumes.* R *there is a glass door which leads into the garden, and a low bay window with a window seat.* UL *a door leads into the hall;* L *are double doors leading into the dining-room.* DS *are easy chairs, a sofa and tables in Regency style. Other items include: a sideboard with glasses; a table with drinks; shelves; paintings on the walls; a telephone; a table lamp and at least one pot plant. A key to the glass door leading into the garden is on the mantelpiece*

When the CURTAIN *rises, the Lights are on revealing the room in total disarray. The sideboard drawers are open and the contents are scattered about the floor. Several anniversary cards and a white alabaster statuette are the only things that remain on the shelves. The glass door* R *is swinging open*

Trevor enters from the garden. He is medium height, late forties, and wearing a lounge suit. He is carrying a golf club. He swings the club apprehensively as he looks around the room

Trevor My God! (*He gives a low whistle. Whispering*) Are you there, John?
John (*off*) In the hall.
Trevor I hope you're ready for this.

John enters. He is also dressed for an evening out. He is the same age as Trevor but a taller, more powerful, figure

John Jesus wept!
Trevor They must have come across the fields and forced a door. Probably took the stuff out this way ... (*He indicates the glass door*)
John The bastards. Look at the footmarks. They didn't even wipe their frigging feet. What sort of homes do they come from?
Trevor They come from the sewers, John. That's where they come from. I see they've taken the Crown Derby and the Delft.

John Yes, and the Wedgwood and the Meissen from the study. And the silver from the dining-room.

Trevor Not the silver. I'm sorry, John.

John They've walked out with my life, Trevor. They've come in here and walked out with my frigging life. I feel personally violated.

Trevor At least they left your golf clubs. If I find one of the bastards do you know what I'm going to do? I'm going to beat the crap out of him, John, then count the strokes.

John That's all they deserve.

Trevor And my God, they'll get it.

John They could be upstairs, I suppose ...

Trevor What? (*He hesitates*) You think they're still here?

John They could be. We did come back early.

Trevor (*lowering his voice*) But they would have heard the taxi, surely?

John Would they care? We are pretty remote here — and there could be several of them. Still, we have one advantage ...

Trevor (*his voice almost a whisper*) What's that, John?

John We're in the right.

Trevor I know we're in the right, John, but first things first. Better call the police — then we'll beat the crap out of them. (*He picks up the phone and listens*) John, the phone's dead. They must have cut the wires.

John I suppose that's normal practice.

Trevor It means we're dealing with professionals — it means we have to be careful. (*He crosses to the hall door, opens it slightly and shouts*) It means we'll have to send the dogs up. Go to the kennels, John, and release the frigging mastiffs. Get the muzzles off the mastiffs, John.

John stares at him and closes the door

John We haven't got any mastiffs, Trevor. We haven't even got a dog.

Trevor They don't know that.

John Do you want to frighten them away?

Trevor Yes. Don't you?

John No. I want to catch the bastards. Mind you, I wish I did have a mastiff, barking mad with rabies. I'd love to see them die slowly, in convulsions, begging for water, unable to drink. And do you know what I'd say? What good's the Georgian silver to you now, you bastards?

Trevor John, I know we're both angry and you feel personally violated but I think we should calm down.

John Calm down! They've spat on my life tonight, Trevor, and you want me to calm down. (*He presses a switch on the bookcase*)

A section of the bookscase swings open to reveal a safe. John turns the dial several times and opens it. He checks the contents, takes out a pistol and closes the safe. Trevor looks astonished

(*Smiling at this*) You didn't know I'd got this, did you?

Trevor I didn't even know you'd got a safe.

John Neither did they. I chose the spot carefully. I knew the illiterate bastards would run a mile from the *Encyclopaedia Britannica*. (*He moves to the hall door*) Well? Are you coming?

Trevor Does it work?

John Of course it works. I use it for killing vermin — so it should be ideal for the purpose. I'll lead the way.

Trevor John, we're forgetting something.

John What?

Trevor (*reverently*) The ladies.

John The ladies?

Trevor Someone has to protect them.

John You're right. You stay with them. I'll go up.

Trevor Be careful.

John They'd better be careful.

Trevor If they are there — what will you do?

John Shoot the shit out of them.

John exits

Trevor looks around. His expression relaxes into a smile

Jenny, Trevor's wife, enters. She looks a few years younger than Trevor. A pretty, fresh-faced woman

Jenny Oh, my God!

Trevor I know. Apparently it's the same in the dining-room and the study. The place is an absolute shambles.

Jenny Poor John. How's he taking it?

Trevor He's got as far as frigging but it could get worse.

Jenny (*curiously*) Why are you smiling?

Trevor I'm not smiling.

Jenny Of course you're smiling.

Trevor Well, I'm smiling now because you said I was smiling but I wasn't smiling before.

Jenny Then what were you doing?

Trevor I don't know.

Jenny You did the same when my mother died and you had to break the news, remember?

Trevor Yes, I sort of pull this face. I suppose it's to conceal my emotions.

Jenny So it's more of a grimace?

Trevor Yes.

Jenny Still looks like a smile. The trouble is the misfortunes of others always seem to put you in such a good humour these days.

Trevor I'm not in a good humour. I'm sorry for him. Poor John; he's not smiling. That vein in his temple's throbbing. I thought he was going to burst a blood vessel.

Jenny Where is he?

Trevor He's gone upstairs.

Jenny Suppose they're up there?

Trevor My money's on John.

Jenny Shouldn't we ring the police?

Trevor The phone's dead.

Jenny That's ominous.

Trevor That's what I thought.

Jenny We're so remote.

Trevor Remote. It's like Wuthering Heights up here. Why couldn't he have lived on a road like anyone else?

Jenny Are you saying he deserved this?

Trevor No but it's times like these when you need neighbours.

Jenny Trevor, you don't even know the name of our neighbours.

Trevor I do, it's ... Marshall.

Jenny They left two years ago. It's Forbes and they haven't spoken to you since you hit their cat with a brick.

Trevor At least we haven't isolated ourselves. That's the trouble with having money; you're so vulnerable to this sort of thing. Makes you wonder if it's worth it.

Jenny Is that why we stayed poor — to avoid being burgled?

Trevor We're not poor — and we had an attempted break-in. And I wish you'd stop trying to imply that I'm jealous of John. He's my oldest friend and I'm proud of his success. He deserves it. He had a rotten childhood; he lived in virtual squalor.

Jenny (*wearily*) Yes, you've told me.

Trevor My mother wouldn't let him in the house. Know why?

Jenny Because he smelled.

Trevor They lived in this slum. I went there once. The room was full of people and it was no bigger than a packing case. And at school ...

Jenny He was bullied.

Trevor I'll say he was. He wore the same pair of trousers for three years. He grew but they didn't. He looked like a bloody giraffe.

Jenny Oh, dear!

Trevor What's the matter?

Jenny They've left the statuette. The one we bought them for their anniversary. That's embarrassing.

Trevor Why?

Jenny They left it, Trevor, because they knew it was a cheap imitation.

Trevor So does Barbara. John put it on the mantelpiece when we arrived. Barbara's been moving it nearer the door ever since. It'll be out of the house by Monday.

Jenny Even so, we can't leave it here — it's too embarrassing. (*She picks up the statuette and looks for somewhere to hide it*)

John enters

John (*gallantly*) Ah, at least they left that. (*He takes the statuette and places it in the centre of the mantelpiece*)

Trevor What's it like up there, John?

John They've been through all the bedrooms. Taken everything of value.

Jenny I'm so sorry, John.

John Do you know one of them actually stretched out on the bed and ate a bag of sweets.

Trevor How do you know?

John There was an impression on the pillow and sweet papers.

Trevor Sounds a cool customer.

Jenny But there was nothing ... untoward?

John Jenny, the bedrooms have been ransacked. What do you mean, untoward?

Jenny There was nothing unpleasant?

John Unpleasant?

Jenny You know ... envy scratches, daubing, that sort of thing.

John No, I didn't see any daubing.

Trevor At least they were professionals.

John Professionals! We haven't had a visit from the Haydn String Quartet, Trevor. They're not professionals. They're crooks. I worked all my life for those things: that's professional. They come and take them: that's frigging stealing!

Trevor Yes, of course. Sorry, John.

Jenny John, don't you think we ought to bring Barbara in now. She must be cold; she's only wearing a thin dress.

John Yes. I don't know how she's going to take this. It's only a year since she was mugged. Where is she?

Jenny In the summer house. I may need some help.

John Why?

Jenny She's asleep.

John (*coldly*) Asleep?

Jenny She's very tired, John.

John Tired. She's as pissed as a fart and you know it. You saw how much she drank at dinner and how quickly. I'm surprised she didn't drink from the bottle to save time. I wouldn't mind but she was the one who undertook to drive.

Trevor She certainly couldn't have done that.

John Neither could any of us. We all drank on the firm understanding that she was going to remain on mineral water. It was because of her that we had to leave the car at the restaurant.

Trevor I think she was drowning her sorrows.

John Well, don't you think it's a shade tactless to be drowning your sorrows on your wedding anniversary? God! What a celebration this is turning out to be.

Trevor Don't worry, John. I'll get her.

Trevor exits

Jenny Poor John. I know how hard you've worked for all this.

John All this? You mean all that. It's gone, Jenny.

Jenny At least they left the pictures ... and there's no damage.

John Perhaps I should be grateful.

Jenny When our neighbours were done they wrote graffiti all over the landscapes and left something unpleasant in the sideboard.

John Ah, but they weren't professional. (*He moves to the drinks table and finds there are no glasses*)

Jenny Did they take any cash?

John No, that's in the safe — they didn't even find it. So they're not that professional. (*He looks for glasses in the sideboard*)

Jenny Is it in this room?

During the following Jenny opens the bookcase to reveal the safe

John (*smiling*) Yes, but I'm not going to tell you where, Jenny. (*He rummages for glasses*) I'm not saying an expert wouldn't have found it, making an intensive search over a long period, but not your average criminal ... (*He turns to see that Jenny has revealed the safe*)

Jenny I thought it might be there ...

John (*frowning*) Yes, well, even if they did find it, it's impregnable. You'd have to know the combination. And no-one knows that except me. (*He closes the bookcase*)

Jenny Not even Barbara?

John No.

Jenny Why not?

John Because the usual way the criminal gets into this sort of safe is by forcing his victim to reveal the combination, often under torture. Since Barbara doesn't know the combination there'd be no point in torturing her.

Jenny But would they know that?

John What?

Jenny That there's no point in torturing her — until they've tortured her?

John (*considering*) I hadn't thought of it like that. I still wouldn't tell her. I carry large sums of money in that safe. And I don't believe in putting temptation in her path, on the grounds that she's totally incapable of resisting it.

Jenny That must infuriate her.

John (*smiling*) It does. The irony is she knows the combination. She knows it but she doesn't know it — if you get my meaning. (*Pause*) I wonder why the alarm didn't go off?

Jenny Perhaps it did.

John No, they'd have heard it at the farm and the cottage. They're our key holders. Barbara probably forgot to set it. (*He begins to straighten the room*)

Jenny Does Barbara usually set it?

John It's her responsibility. I get the car out — she sets the alarm. What do you do?

Jenny We haven't got an alarm. We just leave the lights on ... and the radio ... and sometimes the television. Actually, there's more going on in our house when we're out than when we're at home.

John Did you do that this weekend?

Jenny No, this weekend Trevor left a cup of tea, an open book and a half-eaten sandwich on the kitchen table in sight of the window. He also left a wheelbarrow in the drive and a rake leaning against it at a casual angle, as if a gardening chore had been interrupted. Then, just in case anyone was watching, he drove off down the road and I followed casually in gumboots and he picked me up two streets away ...

John (*staring incredulously*) My God! What's this country coming to?

Barbara enters assisted sympathetically by Trevor. She looks older than Jenny but compensates for this by dressing more elegantly and expensively. At the moment she has the slow solemnity of someone who has had a little too much to drink

Trevor Now, Barbara, you'd better take a deep breath.

Jenny It's not as bad as it looks.

Barbara What isn't?

Jenny I don't think her eyes have adjusted to the light.

John Adjusted to the light! She can't focus. Look at her: she's out to lunch.

Jenny John, please.

John I'm sorry, Jenny, but she was supposed to drive us back, and if she'd done that we'd have had the car and the car phone.

Trevor What about your mobile?
John Strangely enough it's been stolen, Trevor.

Barbara picks up a bottle from the tray

   Haven't you had enough of that?
Barbara No. (*She looks around for glasses*)
Jenny The big thing is no-one's been hurt.
Trevor There's no serious damage.
Jenny No graffiti, no daubing: nothing unpleasant.
Barbara What's she talking about? Where are the glasses? Doesn't anyone
   empty the dishwasher around here?
Trevor What you have to remember is that they're only things.
John They may be only things but they're bloody expensive things.
Trevor I mean they're not as important as people.
John They're more important than some people I can think of — the buggers
   who took them for a start.

Barbara's search for a glass forces her to take in the whole room. She stares

Barbara My God! We've been burgled.
John That's what we've been trying to tell you.
Barbara (*beginning to sober up*) Well, isn't someone going to do some-
   thing? Where are the police?
John You didn't set the alarm, did you?
Barbara How do you know?
John Because the police would have been here.
Jenny Do you remember setting it, Barbara?
Barbara I can't recall ...
John It should be a habit.
Barbara I know, but when a thing becomes a habit you don't always
   remember doing it — which, unhappily, is the story of my life — and even
   if I had set it they're away at the cottage.
John What about the Coopers?
Barbara They're a quarter of a mile away. They probably didn't hear it.
John They didn't hear it because you didn't set it.
Barbara Has the silver gone?
John Yes.
Barbara Crystal?
John Yes.
Barbara Porcelain?
John Yes.
Barbara My jewellery?

John Thought you were wearing it.
Barbara Not all of it.
John Where did you leave it?
Barbara On the dressing-table.
John Then it's gone. Should have been in the safe.
Barbara I can't open the safe.
John You only have to ask.
Barbara You were getting the car out.
John Then you should have worn it.
Barbara All of it? Did you want me to sink to the ground?
John You were doing that anyway.
Barbara Well, I'm not standing here twiddling my thumbs. I'm going to get my car out and fetch the police.
John That'll only slow things down.
Barbara Why?
John Because they'll spend the first half hour breathalysing you.
Trevor I'll go, John. I'm all right. I'll get my car keys. (*He moves to the door*) Jenny, you'd better come and see if there's anything missing ...

Trevor and Jenny exit

John and Barbara glare at each other. Barbara drinks defiantly from the bottle and looks around

Barbara Oh, look, they've left the statuette. Well, that tells us something about them: they've got taste.
John What do you mean?
Barbara I mean they can recognize plaster of Paris when they see it.
John They bought what they could afford. And that means something to me. They are my oldest friends.
Barbara So you keep telling me. Is that why we have them almost every weekend?
John We don't.
Barbara We do. For barbecues, for swimming, for tennis. Almost every weekend. (*Pause*) So he's going to get the car out. That makes a change. I wonder if he'll expect to be reimbursed for the petrol.
John He's not mean.
Barbara He's a freeloader.
John No.
Barbara Then where's his wallet? Have you seen that man's wallet? I haven't. Where does he keep it? I know he keeps making these gestures towards his back pocket. Is it there, do you think?
John There's no need to be sarcastic. He was a friend when I had nothing. I'm not going to lose touch.

Barbara Well, he certainly isn't. I thought he might have offered to pay for the wine tonight but no: all he did was make those feeble gestures towards his backside and then ate all the After Eight mints.

John Look, the meal hasn't cost us anything. It's on the company. I've got them down as visitors from abroad.

Barbara I wish they were — then they'd be going back. Why did you have to ask them down this weekend? It's as if you can't talk to me any more.

John Well, there's more to talk about when there's four of us.

Barbara Oh, yes, she's fascinating. Did you know she makes her own soap?

John What?

Barbara She told me. Well, she doesn't make it, exactly: she recycles it.

John (*staring*) I don't understand. Surely once you've used soap, that's it.

Barbara Not with Jenny. You know all those little pieces of soap that are too small to use? Well, she puts them all in this little gadget — and makes a new piece of soap. (*Pause*) I don't know if she has her own crest but isn't that clever? Probably got the idea from Trevor. It was Trevor who suggested sharing the bath water.

John (*shocked*) Sharing the bath water?

Barbara Since they've been metered they've shared the bath water. Now, I don't know if that means they get in it together — having seen the bath I should have thought that would have been a bit of a squeeze, unless they sit on top of each other — or if they go in one at a time, in which case I'm not sure who goes in first; perhaps they toss for it. But one thing you can say about them: they're not using up a great deal of the world's resources.

John Do you have to be so patronizing? I suppose it's because I knew them before I knew you. It's something you can't share.

Barbara I wouldn't want to.

John You should have known Jenny then. She was so vital, so alive.

Barbara Yes, I wonder what happened.

Trevor enters looking concerned. He is followed by Jenny

John What's the matter, Trevor?

Trevor They've taken my wallet.

Barbara (*interested*) Oh, where was it?

Trevor In my sock.

Barbara (*with a glance at John*) Is that where it was?

Trevor And my credit cards.

Barbara Were they in your sock too?

Trevor Yes. In my suitcase. I didn't think anyone would look in a sock.

Barbara I certainly wouldn't.

Jenny A sock is the first place they'd look, Trevor. Why didn't you carry them with you?

Barbara Yes, I wondered that.

John (*frowning*) Because he didn't think he'd need them. Did you lose anything else?

Trevor My diary.

Barbara Was that in your sock?

Trevor No, on the dressing-table.

Jenny Well, I don't suppose that's important.

Barbara Unless they find your address and burgle you.

Trevor Do you think that's likely?

Barbara Anything's possible. They could steal your engagements, take up with your friends.

John It's not funny, Barbara. At least Trevor knows what it's like now.

Trevor (*stiffly*) I know what it's like, John. We did have the attempted break-in.

Jenny Yes, actually, Trevor was quite resourceful.

Trevor I wouldn't say that.

Barbara What happened?

Trevor I heard this scratching at the landing window one night. I sneaked a look and saw this man on a ladder trying to force an entry.

John What did you do?

Trevor Well, I had nothing on at the time.

Barbara You sleep with nothing on?

Trevor Yes.

Barbara Is that for economy?

John (*warningly*) Barbara.

Trevor I find it more comfortable. Although of course, it did put me at a disadvantage. So I drew the curtains back suddenly and went "Arggh!" (*He makes a full frontal gesture*)

Barbara You did what?

Trevor I went "Arggh!" (*He repeats the gesture*)

John That must have given him a shock.

Jenny It certainly did. He fell from the ladder and ran off down the street.

Barbara I think I'd have done the same.

John Have you lost anything, Jenny?

Jenny Yes, a gold locket.

John Where was it?

Jenny In a jar of face cream.

Trevor I didn't know you had a gold locket.

Jenny I haven't now. It was Mother's.

Trevor Why didn't you wear it?

Jenny Because it didn't go with what I had on.

John Look, we're wasting time. Trevor, did they leave your car keys?

Trevor Yes.

John Then drive down to the farm and call the police. If the Coopers aren't in carry on until you come to a phone box. I'm going to check the lane. I've a feeling they may still be out there. Barbara, you'd better start preparing a list of what's missing.

John exits into the garden

Barbara He's so masterful, isn't he?
Trevor (*moving to follow John*) I'll get the car.
Jenny (*worried*) Trevor, you didn't keep your pin numbers with your credit cards, did you?
Trevor No.
Jenny That's something I suppose.
Trevor They were in my diary.

He exits

Barbara (*smiling*) Well, the old cashpoint's going to get a good thrashing, tomorrow, Jenny. Alarm bells will be ringing at Barclays. Should we start in the study?

She exits followed by Jenny

The room is silent for a moment. The silence is broken by a muffled groan. The cupboard under the window seat flies open and a body rolls out on to the carpet. The body lies there in a crumpled heap. It belongs to a man about fifty. This is Spriggs. He is wearing a mac and pink "Marigold" gloves

Spriggs Gordon Bennet!

Spriggs gradually unwinds himself and stands with difficulty. His head is twisted to one side due to his prolonged confinement. His arm is bent and one of his legs has gone to sleep. He moves forward only to collapse. He strikes his leg furiously and makes his twisted way towards the set of Encyclopaedia Britannica. *He regards them thoughtfully*

Trevor appears outside the garden door, staring in at Spriggs

Spriggs becomes aware of Trevor and plunges his gloved hands into his pockets

Trevor (*entering the room*) Who are you?
Spriggs (*sharply*) Police. And I'll ask the questions. Are you the owner?

Trevor No, I'm a visitor.

Spriggs Oh, yes? What's your name?

Trevor Farrington. Trevor Farrington.

Spriggs Any identification?

Trevor Pardon?

Spriggs Anything to substantiate that you're the said Trevor Farrington?

Trevor (*tapping his pockets*) Er, no.

Spriggs I find that rather strange.

Trevor They stole my wallet.

Spriggs You were mugged?

Trevor No, it was in my sock.

Spriggs Most people carry them in their inside pocket.

Trevor It was in my suitcase.

Spriggs I see. So we don't really know who you are?

Trevor Mr Miles can vouch for me.

Spriggs But he's not here, is he?

Trevor No, he went across the field ...

Spriggs Hm ... (*He turns to look out of the window and tugs furtively at the gloves. All that happens is that the fingers grow longer*) So all we have so far is an unidentified man with no credentials acting in a suspicious manner.

Trevor Look, I can soon —— (*He moves to the hall door*)

Spriggs (*fiercely*) Don't leave this room.

Trevor I was going to get Mrs ——

Spriggs I said don't leave. I don't want you hooking it. I'm not as fast as I was.

Trevor Is there something wrong with your neck?

Spriggs I should be on sick leave.

Trevor Why do you think I'm acting in a suspicious manner?

Spriggs You have a furtive expression, you lick your lips too much and people who enter houses without any means of identification are usually criminals: apart from which your face is familiar.

Trevor I can't help that. And my mouth's dry because we've been drinking. And if I seem furtive it's because you're so suspicious.

Spriggs Of course I'm suspicious. Suspicion is my trade. No means of identification ... I bet you haven't even got a label in that jacket.

Trevor Yes, I have. (*He opens the jacket and shows Spriggs the label*)

Spriggs (*peering closely*) Oh ... You shop there, do you?

Trevor Well, that's not a crime, is it?

Spriggs No, but it hardly goes with this place does it?

Trevor I'm a visitor.

Spriggs So you keep saying. Look, it's not just the obvious fact that you're out of your depth here. And it's not what you've said — it's what you haven't said. You haven't asked me for my ID. A criminal rarely does; he knows a copper when he sees one. You have submitted yourself to this interrogation without question — almost meekly. I could be anyone but you assumed I was a policeman. And why? Guilt. You have a criminal's innate fear of authority.

Trevor All right. Show me your ID.

Spriggs (*sharply*) It's a little late for that now, sunshine. (*He turns to look around the room, pulling frantically at one of his gloves. It stretches and comes off with a loud slap. He turns*) Have you touched anything in here?

Trevor I'm afraid we all have.

Spriggs At the moment I'm more concerned with you.

Trevor Wouldn't they have worn gloves?

Spriggs Are you trying to teach me my job?

Trevor No, but surely ...

Spriggs They may have worn gloves; they almost certainly wore gloves. What we hope for is a moment's aberration, a hole in the finger — something. That's what police work's all about: grinding, soulless routine and a little bit of luck.

Trevor How did you know about the burglary?

Spriggs What?

Trevor How did you know?

Spriggs We had an alarm call put through to the station by a neighbour.

Trevor So Mrs Miles did set the alarm after all.

Spriggs It would appear so.

Trevor Look, I'll just get her ——

Spriggs Never mind about her! I'm going to take a look around the grounds. Stay here. I don't want you disturbing anything.

Trevor You're leaving me here?

Spriggs Yes.

Trevor I thought you suspected me.

Spriggs What made you think that?

Trevor Your attitude.

Spriggs Years in the Force, I'm afraid. But my years of experience tell me that although you have an unfortunate manner and your eyes are a little too close together you haven't got the necessary bottle to make a criminal. Besides which, I think this was done by the Bradford gang. They've been active in this area. Now, whatever your faults, sir, you certainly don't come from Bradford. (*He moves to exit into the garden*)

Trevor One moment, I still haven't seen your ID ...

Spriggs (*hesitating, then smiling*) You're improving, sir. (*He flashes a pocket folder in Trevor's direction*) Inspector Bostock, County CID.

Trevor Look, let me get Mrs Miles.

Spriggs Don't touch that door handle!

Trevor Then how do I get out?

Spriggs You don't. I'll get to Mrs Miles shortly. (*He moves towards the garden once more*)

Trevor Is there something wrong with your leg as well?

Spriggs Yes. I was kicked in the balls by a very nasty piece of work on Friday night. (*He pauses by the door*) Did you say Mr Miles was out there?

Trevor Yes.

Spriggs I'll have a word with him.

Trevor Be careful.

Spriggs Why?

Trevor He's armed.

Spriggs (*closing the door carefully*) What's he got?

Trevor An old army pistol, I think.

Spriggs Would he use it?

Trevor I think he's looking forward to it.

Spriggs (*sighing*) That's all I need. An outraged householder with an old army pistol. It gets more dangerous every year. It used to be antique swords and Gurkha knives — now it's firearms. We're facing an escalation of violence. Well, if you see him first tell him if he tries using it he'll do more time than the burglar.

Trevor And more if he shoots a policeman.

Spriggs (*staring*) Policeman?

Trevor You.

Spriggs Right. They'd throw the key away. (*He crosses to the hall door*)

Trevor Aren't you going to have a word with him?

Spriggs Not at the moment. (*He takes out a spray and squeezes it into his mouth, inhaling noisily*)

Trevor What's that for?

Spriggs Breathing problems and chronic angina.

Trevor You are in a state, aren't you?

Spriggs This job's very ageing. It's the daily confrontation with the worst elements of society, forever contemplating the scabrous face of evil. I know policemen of forty who'd pass for geriatrics. I myself am undergoing counselling.

Trevor Really?

Spriggs Still, goes with the territory, I suppose. (*He opens the hall door*)

Barbara and Jenny enter unexpectedly

Ah. Good-evening, ladies.

Barbara Who are you?

Trevor This is Inspector ... er ...

Spriggs (*beaming*) Chief Inspector Barret.

Trevor (*staring*) Barret?

Spriggs Do I have the pleasure of addressing Mrs Miles?
Barbara Yes.
Spriggs Well, first of all, Mrs Miles: can you vouch for this man?
Barbara Vouch for him?
Spriggs Can you vouch for his character? He say's he's a visitor.
Barbara Well, he is a visitor, but, of course, I can't vouch for his character.
Trevor Barbara!
Jenny Well, I can. He's my husband and he's never done a dishonest thing in his life.
Spriggs How very rare. I didn't realize I was dealing with a paragon of virtue.
Jenny Surely you don't suspect Trevor?
Trevor Of course he doesn't. Actually, he thinks it's the Bradford gang.
Barbara The Bradford gang? Why don't they stay in Bradford?
Spriggs (*sighing*) Because then they wouldn't be known as the Bradford gang, would they? But don't let's be too hasty. I said it could be the Bradford gang. I have to keep an open mind.

Barbara picks up the bottle

Try not to disturb anything, madam.
Barbara Disturb anything! It's been disturbed. I've never seen this house so disturbed. But I'll tell you one thing, it's not as disturbed as I am.
Spriggs There may be fingerprints on that bottle.
Jenny (*acidly*) I don't think there'd be room. Mrs Miles has handled it a great deal this evening.
Barbara (*glaring*) I wouldn't mind, officer, but we've been home all the weekend. We only slipped out for a couple of hours.
Spriggs That's all it needs. I know of a couple who spent a year abroad: came home to find the house exactly as they left it. Popped out for a pizza and got done.
Trevor I suppose it's just your luck.
Spriggs Perhaps. But where the Bradford gang's concerned luck doesn't come into it. They would have had this house under observation.
Barbara You mean this weekend?
Jenny That gives me a cold feeling.
Spriggs Don't be alarmed. I said it could be the Bradford gang. I can't commit myself to one line of enquiry. I need to use my powers of observation dispassionately ... (*He begins to prowl impressively about the room casting odd, cautious glances out of the window*) It's amazing what secrets the scene of the crime can reveal to a practised observer ... (*He sniffs*) The faint aroma of cheap after-shave for example; it pervades the room ... patchouli oil, redolent of the underworld.
Trevor Er, that's me.

Spriggs (*staring*) Is it? (*He sniffs*) So it is ... (*He continues prowling*) We shall of course require a complete list of the items stolen, madam.

Barbara What's the point — you won't get them back.

Spriggs Don't be too sure. No matter how clever these people are they eventually make a mistake.

Trevor There's a large footprint in the flowerbed.

Spriggs (*surprised*) Is there? Well observed, sir. We'll have a cast of that. Large, you say?

Trevor Yes.

Spriggs Could be the Bradford gang. They are well-known for their large feet — although they can move with astonishing rapidity and grace. Anything else you can tell me?

Jenny They've cut the telephone wires.

Spriggs That sounds like them.

Trevor And they've immobilized the cars.

Jenny Oh, no!

Spriggs That was to prevent you raising a hue and cry, sir. They leave nothing to chance. I think we're building up a profile here. (*He takes out a bag of sweets*) Anyone for a barley sugar?

Jenny (*taking one*) Thank you.

Barbara (*taking one*) Er, thank you.

Trevor (*taking one*) Thanks.

At least one sweet paper ends up on the floor

Spriggs I find them most refreshing in these situations: full of energy, and they help with my breathing.

Jenny Do you think you'll catch them, Inspector?

Spriggs I hope so. I've been after them a long time. It would be the pinnacle of my career. But I must keep a clear head. I must assemble the facts with geometric precision. Unfortunately the trouble with geometric precision is it can lead to a conclusion that's absolute codswallop. That never happens to Sherlock Holmes. He can say, "I deduce from the man's clothing that he has recently returned from India — that he's served in the army — rides regularly and is partial to snuff." It never turns out that he's wearing some other bugger's clothes.

They all laugh

John enters from the garden. He is holding the pistol. He stares suspiciously at Spriggs

Ah. There you are, sir.

John Who are you?
Trevor This is Chief Inspector ...
Spriggs Bostock.

Trevor stares

> Would you put that gun away, sir. We are in a confined space and I don't want any accidents. I'll see the licence for it later.

John hesitates, then slips the gun into his pocket

> Did you see any sign of them, sir?
John No.
Spriggs There seem to be two alternatives. Either they've gone across the moors or they could be heading for the motorway.
John Well, aren't you going after them?
Spriggs Wheels have been set in motion. There could, of course, be a third alternative.
John What's that?
Spriggs Did you ever see *Jaws*, sir?
John *Jaws*?
Spriggs They were all looking out to sea, all eyes peeled for the big shark. All searching the horizon — and what happens? It comes round behind them, in the backwater where the children are playing, where they thought they were safe, and starts gobbling.
Jenny Oh!
John What are you suggesting?
Spriggs Have you searched the house thoroughly?
John Well, yes.
Spriggs The attic, the cellar?
John Well, no.
Spriggs Then I suggest you start. I'll search the outhouses. (*He moves to the garden door*)
Trevor Suppose we find someone?
Spriggs Then I empower you to make a citizen's arrest.

> *He exits into the garden*

John (*staring after him*) That's funny.
Trevor What?
John I didn't see his car.
Jenny Probably hid it so as not to alarm the burglars.
Barbara I don't know why he bothered — he's alarmed everyone else.

John What's the matter with his neck?

Trevor He was kicked in the balls by a nasty piece of work on Friday night.

Barbara He doesn't look in very good shape.

Trevor No, and he seemed to have trouble remembering his name. I could have sworn he said Bostock and then Barret.

John How did he know about the robbery?

Trevor The neighbours reported the alarm going off.

John That's strange because I've been down there: the Coopers aren't in. How could they have heard it?

Barbara They couldn't because I didn't set it.

John You said you couldn't remember.

Barbara Well, now I remember.

John picks up a sweet paper and stares

John My God! Sweet papers. He's the one! Don't you see? He's the frigging burglar! (*He takes out the revolver*) Come on, Trevor.

John dashes out

Trevor hesitates, picks up the golf club and hesitates again

Trevor There may be more of them out there. You'd better come with me Jenny. And get something to protect yourself with ...

He exits

Jenny moves to follow Trevor. She hesitates at the door looking for some sort of a weapon. Barbara smiles sweetly and hands her the statuette

CURTAIN

SCENE 2

The drawing-room. Half an hour later

Jenny enters from the garden with the statuette, which she places on a shelf

Barbara enters from the hall. She is drinking from a tumbler

Jenny (*excitedly*) We've caught him.

Barbara Oh, good.

Jenny He was hiding in the summer house. We heard him wheezing.

Barbara I must say he's terribly out of condition for a housebreaker. You'd have thought he'd have chosen something more sedentary ... (*She moves the statuette almost out of sight*)

Trevor and John march Spriggs into the room; John is pointing the gun and Trevor is holding Spriggs by the arm

John Sit down there.

Spriggs You'll be in serious trouble for this.

John Who are you?

Spriggs I've told you — Chief Inspector Dermot.

Trevor That's the third different name!

John Why were you hiding in the summer house?

Spriggs I wasn't hiding. I was searching for clues.

John Under four deck chairs and a sun lounger?

Spriggs If that's where the clues are, that's where you'll find me. Clues don't jump up and bite you, you have to look for them. That's what police work's all about. The painstaking sifting of the evidence, the back-breaking routine ——

Trevor Don't start that again!

Barbara Why did you come here?

Spriggs In answer to your alarm.

Barbara I didn't set it. I forgot.

Spriggs How can you remember you forgot?

John What made you think this man was a policeman, Trevor?

Trevor He showed me his warrant card. It had his picture on it.

John Jenny, search his pockets.

Trevor (*pointing*) That one.

Jenny fishes nervously in Spriggs' pocket and takes out a leather folder

That's it.

Jenny (*examining the folder*) And you recognized this picture?

Trevor I didn't get a good look but it seemed familiar.

Jenny It should do — it's you.

Trevor What?

Jenny It's your office security card — and these are your credit cards.

Trevor (*taking the cards*) My God!

John Now perhaps you'll give us your name.

Spriggs I've given you three: how many do you want?

Jenny How many names have you got?

Spriggs I don't know. I usually say the first thing that comes into my head.

I called myself de Haviland the other day. I mean: do I look like a de Haviland?

John You certainly don't. You look exactly what you are. A mean, pathetic, little crook.

Spriggs Wait a minute. He was prepared to believe I was a policeman.

Trevor You were very convincing.

Spriggs Thank you.

Trevor Do you always say you're a policeman?

Spriggs No, I improvise. Like the time I lifted this emerald ring from a jewellers'. I was across the road when they stopped me. Was I dismayed? No. I told them I wanted to see what it looked like in the daylight.

Trevor Across the other side of the road?

Spriggs (*grinning*) I said the light was better there.

John And they believed you?

Spriggs I can be very persuasive.

John Well, you won't talk your way out of this. And I wouldn't try anything — this gun is loaded.

Spriggs (*sighing*) I knew we'd get back to that. Why don't you put it away? Apart from the fact that it stifles conversation, you don't need it. I'm a sick man. (*He gets busy with his spray*) Chronic angina. High blood pressure. I couldn't get away — and even if I did I couldn't manage those hills. I was raised on the flat. It's all right for the people around here; they've got bigger lungs. They'd soon catch me. That's my trouble. I'm an urban figure in a rural landscape. What chance have I got?

Jenny You've very articulate for a burglar.

Spriggs I know. I spend most of my days in public libraries.

John (*angrily*) Yes, and most of your nights in private frigging houses.

Spriggs Please, don't shout, sir — any sudden attack ... could prove fatal ...

John All right, you're a sick man but how do we know your friends aren't still out there?

Spriggs (*smiling*) Still out there! You've got the noble brotherhood wrong if you think that. They'll be well away. It's like a mission behind enemy lines: every man for himself. They'll be halfway down the motorway by now.

John Yes and with my property.

Barbara Our property.

John Our property and I want it back.

Spriggs Well, what do you want me to do about it? Take an advert in the "Burglars' Weekly"? I shan't see them again. I'll be in prison.

John But you know who they are.

Spriggs I know very little about them. Only that they're proud men deeply ashamed of what they're doing. They've been forced into it by economic necessity — victims of the recession. They led perfectly respectable lives once.

John And what about you? What's your excuse?

Spriggs I never trained. I was misled by political promises. They told me it was a new age, that I was born into a world of leisure. I didn't know they meant unemployment.

John You think that's a sufficient excuse? I could put a bullet into you right now.

Spriggs I wish you'd calm down, sir. This is a highly volatile situation and that vein in your temple's throbbing. Look, you won't get any aggravation from me. It's not my style. Ask anyone. "When apprehended Greasy Spriggs offers no resistance and attempts to talk his way out of it." It's on the file.

Trevor So that's your real name!

Spriggs (*with a sly grin*) Wanna bet?

John Why Greasy?

Spriggs There's a legend that I was once locked in a garage by the owner of the house and that I took all my clothes off, covered my body in multi-grade and exited through the cat flap.

John I don't believe it.

Spriggs I was slimmer in those days.

John It's probably more to do with your slippery nature, Spriggs. Do you know what I'd do with people like you? For the first offence I'd cut off your left hand. For the second offence I'd cut off your right. And if that didn't cure you ——

Spriggs I don't want to know what you'd cut off next.

John I think you'd agree it would reduce crime.

Spriggs It would certainly reduce the demand for gloves. There wouldn't be much call for them around our way. The trouble is one half of the country seems to be robbing the other half. It's bound to cause resentment. My solution is to take it in turns. One half robs Monday, Wednesday and Friday. The other half robs Tuesday, Thursday and Saturday. And we all have Sunday off to enjoy our possessions.

John (*grimly*) Are you mocking me?

Spriggs No. I make it a rule never to mock a man with a gun in his hand.

Trevor I wouldn't get too emotional, John. He's not worth it. Besides you can always get it back on the insurance.

Spriggs And more.

John What?

Spriggs Did you know that insurance claims exceed the value of property stolen by fifty per cent? Get in there, sir: it's your birthday. If you need any receipts ...

John (*angrily*) How dare you? Do you think I'd descend to your level? Don't you understand? Those things are mine and I want them back.

Spriggs But do you really understand the nature of property? Do you really believe we own anything? The Aborigines don't.

John (*incredulously*) What has this to do with the Aborigines?

Spriggs They find the whole idea of ownership laughable. They believe that property is theft.

Barbara Yours certainly is.

Spriggs They know they're going to die, and they know you can't take it with you.

Barbara If my husband can't take it with him he's not going.

John I don't want to take it with me, Spriggs, I just want it while I'm here.

Spriggs In a hundred years' time total strangers will be handling your property.

John They're handling it now, Spriggs. Trevor, go and get a strong rope from the garage.

Trevor What are you going to do?

John We're going to tie him to the chair.

Barbara That's a relief; I thought you were going to hang him.

John You're not going to wriggle out of this one, Greasy.

Trevor exits

Spriggs Do you have to do that, sir? Only I have a sensitive skin — apart from which I can't bear to be restrained.

Barbara Then you've certainly chosen the wrong profession.

Spriggs Can't you reason with him, lady? I've got chronic angina. Suppose I need to reach for my tablets. All I was doing was trying to point out the transient nature of possession. One day this house will echo to unknown voices; there'll be alien laughter from the tennis court; children yet unborn will play in that pool. Strangers will live here.

Barbara Well, if they do, Spriggs, they will have bloody well paid for it. And I don't care if he trusses you up like a chicken.

Spriggs My God! I thought you were supposed to be the weaker sex.

John My wife was mugged last year and relieved of a sapphire and diamond butterfly brooch worth fifteen thousand pounds; so you can expect little sympathy from her.

Trevor returns with the rope

Tie him to the back of the chair, as tight as you can.

Trevor He ought to be able to breathe ...

John That's not essential.

Spriggs Oh, my God ...

John Barbara, you'd better get back to preparing that list.

Barbara Wouldn't it be quicker if he did it?

John Barbara, please.

Barbara What are you going to do?

John I'll try the Coopers again. Give her a hand, will you, Jenny?

Jenny and Barbara exit

Trevor completes the tying

You'd better take the pistol, Trevor. Know how to use it?
Trevor Yes.
John I'll deal with you later, Spriggs ....

John exits

Spriggs (*uneasily*) I thought that sounded rather ominous, didn't you?
Trevor Yes.
Spriggs Of course I'm used to threats; the big question at the moment is would he use that gun?
Trevor Surely the big question at the moment is would I use it?
Spriggs I already know the answer to that: you wouldn't. But would he?
Trevor He will if you make him angry.
Spriggs I'll try and avoid that in future.
Trevor He has this temper. He never thinks of the consequences. John's the sort of man who's gone through life without ever reading the small print.
Spriggs And you do?
Trevor I've always been more cautious.
Spriggs Well, it doesn't seem to have done him much harm.
Trevor No. And the strange thing is he was such a failure at school.
Spriggs Makes you wonder.
Trevor Yes.
Spriggs You knew him at school then?
Trevor I had to keep an eye on him. I was head boy — and he was bullied.
Spriggs (*staring*) They bullied him?
Trevor He was smaller then.
Spriggs He must have been.
Trevor We never thought he'd become such a big success.
Spriggs What did you become?
Trevor I'm a sort of minor civil servant.
Spriggs What does he do?
Trevor He's the managing director of this large international conglomerate. He started there from school, they expanded and he's never looked back.
Spriggs So you could say he was in the right place at the right time.
Trevor Well, you could say that but he worked for it. He came from literally nothing. I'm proud of him.
Spriggs You're proud of him?

Trevor Yes.

Spriggs Let me get this straight. At school he was a failure and you were a big success, and now the situation's reversed — and you're proud of him?

Trevor Yes.

Spriggs Why don't you admit it? You hate the bastard.

Trevor No, I'm pleased for him.

Spriggs You're repressing it.

Trevor I'm not repressing it. I don't hate him. Why should I?

Spriggs Because you've lost, and there's no such thing as a good loser.

Trevor I'm used to losing.

Spriggs That doesn't mean you have to like it. Let me ask you something. If that bastard had a heart attack — which can't be far off if you ask me — what would be your strongest feeling?

Trevor I'd be sorry.

Spriggs You'd be bloody delighted.

Trevor That's where you're wrong. I'm not jealous of his success because money's never changed John. He's always kept in touch. He's always preferred my company to that of his fancy friends. He's totally unspoilt.

Spriggs Some might take that view; others might see him as a rich bastard who has you around so he can flaunt it.

Trevor No.

Spriggs You're his yardstick, that's all. With you he can measure how far he's come.

Trevor On the contrary it's because he enjoys my company. We do most things together. We swim, we play tennis ——

Spriggs Yes, I've seen you play tennis.

Trevor You've watched us?

Spriggs (*nodding*) This afternoon, from the lane. I was the rustic figure in the pork pie hat, resting on a stick.

Trevor That was you?

Spriggs Yes. I like a sporting contest. Not that it was very sporting and it wasn't much of a contest. Do you always lose?

Trevor He's a good player. What did you mean, not very sporting?

Spriggs He cheats.

Trevor No.

Spriggs He cheats on the line calls.

Trevor No.

Spriggs And he gloats.

Trevor He's never gloated.

Spriggs He does when he's got his back to you — positively gloats. And why do you always have to play at that end?

Trevor Which end?

Spriggs The end with the tree.

Trevor It's only a friendly; we don't bother to change ends.

Spriggs There's nothing friendly about it. He forces you into that tree. You're playing half your shots out of the branches. You'd need to be a bleeding monkey.

Trevor It's not important. It's only a game.

Spriggs It may be only a game but if he cheats at one thing — he'll cheat at another ...

Trevor (*after a pause*) What do you mean?

Spriggs I mean no-one makes all this money without robbing someone.

Trevor No, he had a share option.

Spriggs What's that?

Trevor The company gave him an option to buy shares three years ago — and they went up. He didn't have to find the money and he was able to take the profit.

Spriggs Suppose they'd gone down?

Trevor He wouldn't have had to buy them — it was an option.

Spriggs Is that legal?

Trevor Yes.

Spriggs How much did he make?

Trevor About three million.

Spriggs (*staring*) Three — ! And you're sure it's legal?

Trevor Yes. They didn't want to lose him. They're called golden handcuffs.

Spriggs I know all about handcuffs but I've never come across that variety. You mean he trousered three million quid?

Trevor Yes but no-one got robbed; the shares simply went up in value.

Spriggs Why?

Trevor Because profits went up.

Spriggs Exactly: and do you know why they went up? Because they reduced the work force and put half the production out to subcontractors. So someone got robbed, didn't they?

Trevor Who?

Spriggs The poor sods that got laid off.

Trevor (*curiously*) How do you know all this?

Spriggs I know. Three million. Makes you wonder what's in that safe, Trevor.

Trevor And how did you know about the safe?

Spriggs I know.

Trevor Then why didn't you open it?

Spriggs Who do you think I am — Raffles? That's a Webley 1400. The sight of one of those is enough to make strong men weep.

Trevor Couldn't you have blown it with gelignite?

Spriggs Not my scene, Trevor. Too volatile for the uninitiated. I knew a bloke who tried to blow a Webley 1400. When the smoke cleared the safe was still intact but he was standing stark naked with his dick in his hand.

You need to know the combination. Six figures, something personal to the owner so he won't forget it.

Trevor Yes, I suppose that's important.

Spriggs Certainly is. I know someone with a Webley 1400: forgot the combination — that was twelve years ago — still can't get into it.

Trevor Surely he could call in the manufacturers, get a locksmith.

Spriggs Not really. You see the contents would take some explaining.

Trevor Oh, I see.

Spriggs Every day he tries to remember. It's driving him crazy. He knows it's some sort of date, a moment in history. He's got as far as the Normandy landings but still no joy. Reminds me of that body they found when they were excavating the Temple. Mouthful of gold teeth and died a bankrupt.

Trevor Why was that?

Spriggs Well, he had them as an investment, see. But he made the mistake of insisting on a perfect fit. When the great day came he couldn't get them out.

Trevor What did he do?

Spriggs Shot himself. That's what poverty can do to a man. Don't you ever get tired of being poor, Trevor?

Trevor I'm not poor. (*Pause*) So you'd need to know the combination?

Spriggs Something personal to him.

Trevor Like his date of birth?

Spriggs No, I've tried that.

Trevor How did you know his date of birth?

Spriggs Found his birth certificate. Did you know he was a bastard?

Trevor What?

Spriggs Mind you, I didn't need his birth certificate to tell me that. I'd almost given up when I noticed the cards.

Trevor Cards?

Spriggs Wedding anniversary cards.

Trevor I don't think John would want to remember that.

Spriggs But could he forget it? I know I can't. So I started to try a few combinations; that's how I got trapped. Was the anniversary today?

Trevor Well, yes.

Spriggs And how long have they been married?

Trevor Twenty years.

Spriggs Twenty years! You don't get that for killing someone. So that would be twenty-fifth of October ... Seventy-six. Two ... five ... one ... nought ... seven ... six. I wonder if that's the combination?

Trevor Well, it's too late to find out.

Spriggs Is it? Are you an honest man, Trevor?

Trevor I don't know.

Spriggs No, none of us do until we're tested. Is it honesty or the fear of being caught? How would you like to gamble?

Trevor What do you mean?

Spriggs That we've got the right combination and there's money in that safe. What about it — that money against my freedom?

Trevor You're crazy.

Spriggs Am I? Trevor, that money's ill-gotten. That means it won't be reported and you'll never have a better chance. You won't be suspected: I will. And I'll be gone. Two, five, one, nought, seven, six, Trevor.

Trevor hesitates in front of the bookcase

Trevor I don't even know if there's any money there.

Spriggs No-one has a Webley 1400 to keep his cuff links in. And my sources tell me the figure could be adjacent to a hundred thousand.

Trevor What!

Spriggs Say you left the room for a few minutes and when you came back I was gone.

Trevor No, I couldn't do it to John.

Spriggs He'd do it to you. Two, five, one, nought, seven, six ...

Trevor No.

Spriggs He'd do it to you, and worse ... Two, five, one, nought, seven, six.

Trevor slowly opens the bookcase

Jenny enters

Trevor quickly closes the bookcase

Jenny Barbara says she needs a strong man; they've jammed the drawers in the tallboy.

Trevor What about him?

Jenny I'll stay.

Trevor Are you sure?

Jenny Yes. (*She takes the gun*) I can squeeze a trigger just as well as you.

Spriggs My God! What happened to the gentle sex? I blame those video nasties.

Trevor exits

I thought you'd be more understanding, more compassionate.

Jenny Don't depend on it.

Spriggs Don't you believe in forgiveness?

Jenny What?

Spriggs I know it's an old-fashioned word but don't you believe in giving someone a chance? A last chance. I can't face prison, not again. What's the point? I'll only come out worse than when I went in.

Jenny I find that hard to believe.

Spriggs Whereas, if you were to let me go I swear I'd never re-offend. I swear that on the head of my dying mother.

Jenny (*half-smiling*) Dying mother?

Spriggs She doesn't know it. Lingering illness. Although tonight should speed things up. Shock will probably kill her.

Jenny Spare me the details.

Spriggs No, you don't want to hear, do you? They'll be waiting for me tonight, round the table, looking at that empty chair. My poor mother, my anxious wife, my daughter — pregnant at fifteen — my youngest with learning difficulties ...

Jenny You seem very unfortunate in your choice of relatives.

Spriggs Perhaps you'd like to make that phone call, telling them Dad's going to be late, five years late, the rest of his life late.

Jenny I would do but you've cut the telephone wires.

Spriggs Well, I can't say I'm surprised. No-one's ever believed in me: why should you? If they had, things may have been different. Tell me something: can you put your hand on your heart and say that you've never done anything dishonest?

Jenny I most certainly ... (*She hesitates*)

Spriggs You've just thought of something.

Jenny It's not important.

Spriggs Then why can't you tell me?

Jenny It was a long time ago.

Spriggs There's no statute of limitations on crime.

Jenny It wasn't a crime. It was when I was a student. It was silly really.

Spriggs Yes?

Jenny There was this book stall on the market.

Spriggs Go on.

Jenny It was kept by a one-eyed man. He wore a patch.

Spriggs Only one eye. Sounds promising.

Jenny He had boxes of books. Some at one pound — some at five pound. The book I wanted was the *Oxford Book of English Verse*. It was in the five pound box. Are you with me?

Spriggs With you? I'm ahead of you.

Jenny I was a poor student. Every Saturday I haggled with him over the price but he wouldn't reduce it ...

Spriggs So?

Jenny One lunchtime he went to the pub and left the stall in the charge of a small boy with glasses.

Spriggs Glasses! Good eyesight seems to have been at a premium on that stall.

Jenny While he was gone I took the book from the five pound box and put it in the one pound box and asked the boy in glasses how much it cost.

Spriggs And he said a pound.

Jenny Yes. It was an impulse.

Spriggs Don't you believe it. That was carried out with all the skill and cunning of an international fraud. And by getting four-eyes to name the price you avoided any possibility of retribution. It was flawless.

Jenny It was quite trivial.

Spriggs Trivial? And what happened when the old one-eye got back from the pub, found the book missing and checked his float. Who'd get the blame? I'll tell you: four-eyes. A clip around the ear and instant dismissal.

Jenny I don't suppose he even noticed.

Spriggs You don't think that. Did you ever go back to that stall?

Jenny No.

Spriggs And do you ever quote from the *Oxford Book of English Verse* without thinking of that boy in glasses?

Jenny No.

Spriggs Do you know what it feels like to be wrongfully accused and sent on a downward spiral? I do. That happened to me. I was that little boy with glasses.

Jenny Well, there's nothing I can do about it now.

Spriggs There is. You can right that wrong. You can let me go. Give me a second chance. If I'd been given a second chance all those years ago, life might have been different.

Jenny You mean like the Bishop's candlesticks?

Spriggs (*staring*) Bishop's candlesticks? I wasn't in on that job. I've never robbed the Church.

Jenny No, it's a story. The convict stole the Bishop's candlesticks but he didn't press charges and the man became a respectable citizen.

Spriggs That's my point. What do you say?

Jenny (*hesitating*) If I let you go will you promise never to come back?

Spriggs I promise.

Jenny puts down the pistol and begins to release Spriggs

Jenny And you'll never do this sort of thing again?

Spriggs On my mother's life. (*He straightens up from the chair*)

Jenny Hurry, before someone comes back.

Spriggs God bless you. (*He crosses to the garden door*)

Jenny Wait a minute. Take this. (*She hands him the statuette*)

Spriggs What?

Jenny It's a gift.

Spriggs (*uncertainly*) Oh, thank you. (*He hesitates*)

Jenny What are you waiting for?

Spriggs (*uneasily*) Those things out there, diving and squeaking — are they
  bats?
Jenny Yes, they're catching insects.
Spriggs They get into people's hair, don't they?
Jenny No, that's an old wives' tale.
Spriggs But they are blind, aren't they?
Jenny Yes, that's why they make those little squeaking noises.
Spriggs I'll make little squeaking noises if they get in my hair.
Jenny I mean they have their own radar.
Spriggs So do Phantom jets but they still crash. And suppose I meet one
  that's stopped squeaking, that's got a mouthful of flies? God! I hate the
  country. (*He heads for the hall door*)
Jenny Where are you going?
Spriggs I think I'll leave by the front ...

Barbara enters from the hall

Spriggs moves to put the statuette back on the mantelpiece

Barbara Trevor says can you get his tool kit from the car ... (*She stops and
  stares at Spriggs*) Why is he untied? (*She picks up the pistol*)
Jenny The ropes were hurting him.
Barbara You should be more careful, Jenny. He's as slippery as an eel. Go
  on. I'll take care of him.
Jenny Are you sure?
Spriggs Hang about. Is that wise? She wasn't even allowed to drive the car
  home. If a car's a loaded gun in the hands of a drunk, what's a loaded gun
  — that's what I want to know.
Barbara I'm not drunk. Go on, Jenny.
Jenny I won't be a moment ...

Jenny exits

Barbara regards Spriggs balefully

Spriggs I wish you'd stop waving that about. What does he want a gun for,
  anyway?
Barbara He uses it to shoot rabbits. He says it helps him relax.
Spriggs Well, I must say I've never seen anyone more in need of relaxation
  than your husband, but do you think it works?
Barbara I'm not sure. It certainly relaxes the rabbits.
Spriggs That's what worries me. Well, I'm not a bleeding rabbit and I don't
  like the way that vein's throbbing in his temple and the way he keeps saying
  frigging all the time.

Barbara Would you prefer he used something stronger?

Spriggs No. I'm all for verbal restraint. In my view bad language is only one short step behind physical violence. That's what those Hampstead trendies didn't realize when they encouraged the working classes to swear: now they wonder why they're being knocked down in alleyways.

Barbara If you don't like violence you'd better come and sit down.

Spriggs hesitates and then sits

Spriggs You hate me, don't you? Is it because you've been mugged?

Barbara What do you think?

Spriggs Were you hurt?

Barbara Not really. It was in an underground car park. He came out of the shadows. He snatched my bag — then my necklace and then my ear-rings.

Spriggs And your brooch ...

Barbara Yes. And then he left without a word. I felt like a soldier who'd been stripped of his rank on the parade ground.

Spriggs And that's all that happened?

Barbara Yes, he didn't try to snatch anything else ...

Spriggs Did they catch him?

Barbara No. I didn't even know what he looked like. He wore a balaclava helmet.

Spriggs So you couldn't identify him.

Barbara No. I thought for a moment it might have been my husband trying to get some of his money back. He was about the right height.

Spriggs Does he object to you spending money?

Barbara Don't all husbands?

Spriggs I understand it's the main source of contention between couples.

Barbara He says I'm the black hole in our personal finances. He never even asked me if I'd been hurt; just what was taken.

Spriggs And a diamond and sapphire butterfly brooch had been taken worth fifteen grand.

Barbara Yes.

Spriggs Still, I suppose it was insured.

Barbara Yes but it's not the same, is it? My husband gave it to me on my birthday.

Spriggs So he can be generous.

Barbara Yes, although not as generous as he was. I notice when he makes cheques out these days the pen squeaks more than it did, there's more flourish to the signature and the sound as he rips the perforation is quite deafening.

Spriggs So you don't have your own money?

Barbara You ask a lot of questions, don't you?

Spriggs I'm fascinated by other people's lives.

Barbara Is that why you break into houses?

Spriggs (*rising*) Yes, in a way. I suppose I'm lonely. I come from a broken home. I was a latch-key child. I've always been on the outside, seen the light through the window, heard the laughter. That's why I always wanted to know what was behind the locked door and to share for a short time an intimate existence with other people.

Barbara I don't mind you sharing it, Spriggs, I just don't want you taking it away with you.

Spriggs I suppose that's envy.

Barbara So it's this aching loneliness that makes you burst into people's houses?

Spriggs I don't burst in. I enter with reverence, with a sense of privilege. And it's been a privilege to do this place.

Barbara Really?

Spriggs Everything in such exquisite taste. Some of the rooms — breathtaking. I must compliment you on your sense of colour and style.

Barbara How do you know it's my taste?

Spriggs It's usually the woman. And you're obviously more mature than he is. I suppose that's because you're older.

Barbara (*shocked*) What! How did you know that? I don't look it, do I?

Spriggs (*alarmed*) No! Don't squeeze that trigger, it was only a casual remark. You don't look older: in fact you look younger.

Barbara Then how did you know?

Spriggs I saw your birth certificate.

Barbara What?

Spriggs It was in the escritoire in your dressing-room — in the secret drawer.

Barbara You looked at my birth certificate?

Spriggs I hope you don't mind.

Barbara So you don't just take things. You pry.

Spriggs As I said, I'm fascinated by other people's lives.

Barbara (*moving closer with the gun*) And when you looked in the drawer did you find anything else ...

Spriggs Oh, yes. And since it's something you may not be able to claim for on the insurance, a second time ... I'll return it. (*He fishes into his pocket and produces a brooch*) One diamond and sapphire butterfly brooch — early Victorian, worth fifteen grand. Lost and now found ...

Spriggs hands the brooch to Barbara

Barbara Thank you. (*She regards it thoughtfully for a moment*) Suppose I were to let you go?

Spriggs (*smiling*) I thought you might.

Barbara You'd better go through the garden.

Spriggs (*hesitating*) You won't shoot me, will you? Sort of by accident?

Barbara No — I'm not drunk.

Spriggs I didn't say you were. At least not as drunk as you'd have us believe.

Barbara You'd better hurry.

Spriggs (*pausing by the garden door*) Just one question. Why were you so sure you hadn't set the alarm?

Barbara I remembered not doing it.

Spriggs But if it was absentmindedness how can you be sure? Unless it was deliberate. But that wouldn't make any sense, would it? Or would it?

Barbara Goodbye, Spriggs.

Spriggs Goodbye.

Spriggs turns to the garden door

  John enters from the hall

Barbara turns towards John

John Barbara! He's getting away!

Spriggs turns back from the door

Barbara turns and fires

Spriggs clutches his side and falls

CURTAIN

ACT II

Scene 1

The drawing-room. A few minutes later

Spriggs is sitting in a chair clutching his side with both hands

The others are gathered about him showing various degrees of concern

Trevor Does it hurt?

Spriggs Of course it bloody hurts.

Jenny Can I look?

Spriggs (*sharply*) Are you a doctor?

Jenny No.

Spriggs Then keep away.

Barbara We want to help you.

Spriggs Yeah, help me to an early grave.

Barbara I'm sorry.

Spriggs Sorry! It's a bit late for sorry, isn't it?

Barbara I feel dreadful.

Spriggs You feel dreadful! As soon as I saw that gun I knew it was going to be used. Now look at me. I happen to believe what a noble work is man. I've always considered my body a sacred trust. I've looked after it. Now I find I've one more hole than nature intended. And all because of you.

Barbara I said I was sorry.

Spriggs Well, you can't say it often enough as far as I'm concerned.

John Look, I take full responsibility.

Spriggs Good. Because there's a three-year prison sentence in this for someone — and damages.

John What?

Spriggs I'm not a bloody rabbit. I have rights.

John You were trying to escape.

Spriggs Can you blame me!

Jenny Let me take your jacket off.

Spriggs Don't touch me! I may not be much but I've never shot anyone.

John What did you expect? You break into my house at the dead of night ——

Barbara Our house.

Spriggs What did I expect? I expect you to set me an example. I expect some moral leadership. Instead of which I get gunned down on the bleeding Axminster.

John No-one asked you to come here.

Spriggs Don't worry, I'll wait for an invitation next time in gold lettering.

Barbara It proves one thing — I couldn't kill anyone.

Spriggs Well, you've made a bloody good stab at it, that's all I can say. I'm dying.

John You're talking a great deal for someone who's dying.

Spriggs Why not? I may not have another chance. These may be my last words.

Barbara I only meant to frighten you.

Spriggs Then you succeeded beyond your wildest dreams.

Jenny What worries me is that I can't see any blood.

Spriggs That's because I'm anaemic.

Trevor I thought you had high blood pressure.

Spriggs I have. Any idea what strain that puts on the system? High blood pressure and no blood.

Jenny My worry is that he's bleeding internally.

Spriggs And mine.

Trevor Can we get you something to drink?

Jenny That would be fatal with a stomach wound.

Spriggs I'll take a sip, my mouth's dry.

John It's all that talking.

Jenny I'll get some water.

Spriggs No, vintage port, if you don't mind. If I'm going — I'll go in style.

Jenny pours him a drink

Trevor We should ring for an ambulance.

John The line's been cut.

Trevor Perhaps we could fix it.

John Where was it cut?

Spriggs At the pole, I think. I didn't do it. I can't stand heights.

John Let's take a look, Trevor. Barbara, you'd better rest, you look terrible ...

John and Trevor exit

Barbara Terrible?

She looks concerned and follows

Jenny and Spriggs are left alone

Spriggs Did you hear that? She looks terrible. What about me?

Jenny Well, I must say you're very lively for someone who's dying.

Spriggs Yes, well, I'm functioning entirely on adrenalin at the moment. (*He groans*)

Jenny You really should let me take a look.

Spriggs No — it's too late. Get me a cigarette, would you?

Jenny Yes ... Oh ... There used to be a silver cigarette box on the coffee table ...

Spriggs Did there? I wonder where it went?

Jenny I think there's some in the study. I won't be a moment ...

She exits

Spriggs smiles. He stands up and crosses stealthily to the garden door. He finds it locked. His smile fades. He returns to his glass of port

The sounds of movement can be heard off; someone is returning. Hearing this, Spriggs pours the glass of port down his shirt and studies the effect. He sits

Jenny enters. She gives Spriggs a cigarette

Spriggs Thank you. If you see smoke appearing from an unexpected aperture don't be alarmed.

Jenny I'm glad to see you haven't lost your sense of humour.

Spriggs If I go — I'll go with a merry quip on my lips.

Jenny (*thoughtfully*) You're very brave.

Spriggs We never know what inner resources we have until we need to call on them.

Jenny (*starting*) My God!

Spriggs What's the matter?

Jenny You're beginning to bleed.

Spriggs Am I?

Jenny Let me look.

Spriggs Are you ready for this ...? (*He opens his jacket*)

Jenny (*faintly*) Oh.

Spriggs You wouldn't have made a nurse; I can see that.

Jenny recovers slightly and touches Spriggs' shirt

Jenny It's very pale.

Spriggs I'm very pale.

Jenny studies her finger and then licks it

Jenny It's port!
Spriggs What?
Jenny It isn't blood, it's port. You haven't been shot, you've been
  pretending.
Spriggs I was shot, only it hit my prayer book.

Jenny moves towards the hall door

  Where are you going?
Jenny I'm going to tell them.
Spriggs No, you're not.
Jenny Why not?
Spriggs (*taking a locket from his pocket*) Because of this ...
Jenny My locket.
Spriggs Yes. You couldn't have worn it tonight, could you? Not on their
  anniversary.
Jenny Give it to me.
Spriggs He gave it to you, didn't he?
Jenny What do you mean?
Spriggs I mean a locket usually has two pictures: the woman and her
  beloved. And so has this — but the beloved ain't Trevor.
Jenny What do you want?
Spriggs To get out of here, that's all. Then it's yours.

John enters

John Trevor's getting a ladder ... (*He stops and studies the others*) What's
  the matter?
Jenny (*after a pause*) He's bleeding.
John Oh, no!
Spriggs I'm afraid so.
John Not on the carpet.
Spriggs What?
John Can't we get him into the kitchen? It's a tiled floor in there.
Spriggs Charming.
Jenny I'll get a towel ...
Spriggs Don't rush. I want to talk to Mr Miles ...

Jenny exits

John and Spriggs regard each other for a moment

John Still talking, Spriggs? I should have thought you'd want to save your
  breath.

Spriggs I just wanted to say ... if I were to die ...

John Yes?

Spriggs It's going to look very bad for you.

John Worse for you, I'd imagine.

Spriggs Perhaps you don't care what happens to your wife.

John Why do you say that?

Spriggs She could get into serious trouble. You both could. Shooting someone with an unlicensed gun.

John What makes you think it's unlicensed?

Spriggs Guns of that age usually are. Not going to look very good: managing director in shooting incident. Doesn't inspire business confidence. Get my drift?

John Yes.

Spriggs Now the important thing is to put as much distance between myself and this house as soon as possible.

John How can you do that? You're wounded.

Spriggs I'll manage.

John They're still out there, aren't they?

Spriggs Possibly, but not for long. They're city dwellers. The countryside makes them nervous. And there are those eyes ...

John What eyes?

Spriggs All those eyes: every time you flash a light, there they are, yellow and green, staring at you through the bushes.

John They're probably deer.

Spriggs I don't care what they are. It's bleeding intimidating. Why don't our eyes light up like that?

John I've no idea.

Spriggs Good thing I suppose. It would make floodlit football out of the question. Imagine five thousand pairs of eyes lighting up in the main stand. Frightening. God! I hate the countryside.

John No-one asked you to come.

Spriggs You're right. And if you just tell me where the key to the door is ... I'll make myself scarce ...

John It's on the mantelpiece ...

Spriggs moves to the mantelpiece

I didn't say you could take it. I'm thinking ...

Spriggs Well, don't leave it too long. (*Uneasily*) What are you thinking?

John I'm thinking why is it that you're holding your side when the bullet's embedded up there in the plaster? (*He indicates a mark on the wall*)

Spriggs (*following John's gaze*) What?

John By the window.

Spriggs Must have ricocheted.

John You mean it bounced off you? My God! What are you made of, Spriggs? You must have a hide like a rhinoceros.

Spriggs All right. (*He sits wearily*) It was worth a try, wasn't it?

John Don't try and bluff a bluffer, Spriggs. I've had men like you for breakfast. And no matter how much you wriggle, you're staying. I'm going to lock you in the cellar.

Spriggs No!

John You're a greasy, devious little toad, Spriggs. I don't trust you.

Spriggs Can't we be civilized about this?

John But you're not civilized, are you?

Spriggs I am. I have standards. I have my parameters. I wouldn't rob a church.

John Well, I imagine that's fairly uncommon.

Spriggs Don't you believe it. I know of a certain stained glass window — much admired, Ascent of Lazarus — which is now gracing a Tokyo restaurant. And I know of another geezer who has a medieval font on his patio stuffed with geraniums. Now that's what I call a decline in moral standards.

John Don't tell me you're religious!

Spriggs Yeah, Anglican. I don't go as often as I should — and I am in dispute over women priests but ——

John But you're a frigging thief, Spriggs.

Spriggs Well, no-one's perfect.

John Thou shalt not steal.

Spriggs Yes but that's only one out of ten, isn't it? I haven't worshipped any graven images. I haven't coveted my neighbour's ass, or his ox, or his ... wife ...

They regard each other for a moment

John Perhaps we should be grateful.

Spriggs Well, let's face it, everyone's on the make these days, aren't they? What about these directors of privatized companies voting themselves fat pay rises. And who are they? Just civil servants who got lucky. And what about those water boards, hey? Hundreds of millions in dividends last year and now they want to meter our water — and that comes from God!

John It has to be filtered.

Spriggs That's the trouble: everything that comes from God gets filtered.

John Look, if you feel like that, rob them, not me.

Spriggs (*with an evil grin*) Don't worry, I will. I've got their addresses. In the meantime, you're not doing so badly. What about those share options? What a nice little earner — and all perfectly legal.

John Exactly. And that's the difference between you and me.

Spriggs No. The only difference is you don't have to wear a mask. You can do it barefaced. Three million.

John That money was earned.

Spriggs But not by you. By those poor buggers you laid off. What I want to know is when you've laid everyone off who's going to buy the bleeding goods?

John Don't tell me you're an economist as well as a philosopher. There's still employment; the work is simply subcontracted to reduce overheads.

Spriggs Subcontracted! Do me a favour. You mean some family sweatshop in Birmingham with Granny turning out washers in the outhouse. No, what I'm saying is: since the unemployed earned this money in the first place, and since I'm unemployed, I'm sort of entitled.

John What!

Spriggs What I'm involved in here is a redistribution of wealth, that's all.

John So you're not a criminal after all, Spriggs: you're Robin Hood.

Spriggs No, I don't give it to the poor. I merely keep trying to point out the ephemeral quality of money. One day you've got it, the next day it's gone.

John It is when you've been around. You don't really believe all that garbage. It's a one-sided argument and you know it.

Spriggs Of course it's a one-sided argument. You don't expect me to take your side as well, do you? If the truth's known we're all as bad as each other.

John I'm as bad as you?

Spriggs I blame it on our forebears. Once upon a time the old caveman would grab a piece of meat with both hands and gnaw it to death in a corner. Then one day he found he could eat out of one hand and hold another piece for later. That's when the first merchant banker was born.

John You dare to compare yourself with me? (*He rises angrily*)

Spriggs Sorry. I didn't mean to annoy you. Actually, I was trying to steer the conversation into calmer waters. The trouble is, when I'm confronted with a gun I do tend to gabble.

John Well, I don't want to hear any more. Society has its rules and I abide by them.

Spriggs Are you sure?

John What do you mean?

Spriggs I mean: what's in that safe?

John (*guardedly*) What safe?

Spriggs The safe behind the *Encyclopaedia Britannica* — my favourite reading as a matter of fact.

John How did you know about that?

Spriggs I know. A Webley 1400. A Rolls Royce amongst safes. No-one uses that to keep the housekeeping in. The talk is there's over a hundred grand in there.

John Talk! What talk? Where?

Spriggs Amongst the denizens of the underworld.

John You mean I'm being watched?

Spriggs Of course you're being watched. You're all being watched. In fact, it's a good thing our eyes don't shine in the dark, otherwise when you put your lights on you'd see so many gleaming eyeballs out there you'd be dazzled. (*He moves to the safe*) Now, I'm not a businessman but I have to ask myself: why keep a large amount of money in a safe when it could be earning interest?

John Perhaps I have to make some large cash payments.

Spriggs You mean to certain Third World gentlemen to grease the wheels of commerce?

John Something like that.

Spriggs It's nothing like that. That money isn't going out, it's coming in. From our friend the grateful subcontractor.

John You don't know that.

Spriggs I do because it was an embittered subcontractor who told me.

John Embittered. Yes, because I wouldn't accept shoddy work. The work has to be first class. So if it were true and I deny everything, the company doesn't suffer. So who's losing?

Spriggs Well, the Inland Revenue for a start.

John (*grabbing Spriggs*) You're going in the cellar.

Spriggs No, don't do that, guv. I don't like cellars: they're too Gothic for my taste. Look, I was only speculating. I won't say a word. Honest. After all, I didn't tell Trevor you were having it off with his wife, did I?

John (*appalled*) What?

Spriggs I said you were being watched. I'm not judging you. I can understand it. A man of your obvious virility married to an older woman. Bound to be tempted — stands to reason.

John Spriggs, if you so much as breathe a word of what you've just said, not only will I deny it but I'll make you regret you ever ... (*He stops and stares*) What do you mean an older woman? She's not an older woman.

Spriggs Well, I don't suppose some people would think five years is important, but ——

John Five years. What are you talking about? My wife's a year younger than I am.

Spriggs Is she?

John Yes.

Spriggs Not according to her birth certificate.

John You've seen her birth certificate?

Spriggs Yes. Haven't you? No, I can see you haven't. It was in the escritoire, in the secret compartment.

John What secret compartment? What are you talking about?

Spriggs Oh dear. I hope I haven't let the cat out of the bag. I don't want to
be guilty of destroying any illusions here. Only when I compared it with
yours.

John With mine?

Spriggs With your birth certificate. And I'm sorry about your unfortunate
start in life but there's no shame in it, is there?

John You've been going through our private papers.

Spriggs Not to satisfy any vulgar curiosity, I assure you. And I could have
been mistaken ... She's a fine looking woman. And no-one looks her best
at this time of night ...

John (*blankly*) Five years?

Spriggs Well, as I said I could be wrong but I did see it in black and
white — and what can't speak can't lie.

Trevor enters

Trevor I couldn't repair the wires but I wondered: perhaps we could put him
on the motor mower and trundle him down to the village. John?

John Five years.

Trevor John, are you all right?

John Five bloody years, Trevor.

Trevor No, three.

John Three?

Trevor That's what he said. But it wouldn't come to that. No court would
convict you — either of you. Now, if we put him on the mower ——

John There's no need.

Trevor What?

John He hasn't been shot. The bullet's up there in the plaster.

Trevor But he said ——

John I know what he said but he's a liar. (*Slowly*) So don't believe anything
he tells you. Anything.

Trevor Don't worry, I won't.

Spriggs That's right, Trevor, you believe him — like you believe his line
calls.

John Line calls. What's he talking about?

Trevor He's watched us play tennis.

John And?

Trevor He says you cheat.

John Cheat!

Trevor He says you call the ball out when it's in.

John I see. And what do you think?

Trevor I don't think you cheat.

John I should think not.

Trevor But you do call the ball out when it's in.

John What!

Trevor You see I hit the ball with a lot of swerve. It starts out but at the last moment it goes in.

John Does it? Well, as far as I'm concerned it starts out and at the last moment it stays out.

Trevor If you say so.

John Not if I say so. I always call them as I see them, Trevor.

Trevor Perhaps you don't see them very well.

John Trevor, what's come over you? We've never gone in for gamesmanship.

Spriggs Then why does he have to play under the tree?

Trevor Yes, why do I have to play under the tree?

John What tree?

Trevor The tree at the end of the court. The giant chestnut. My God! You can't miss it.

Spriggs quietly moves to the mantelpiece and takes the key, then heads silently towards the window

John Look, you don't have to play under the tree. I'll play under the tree. I wasn't even aware of the tree.

Trevor No? Then what about the tree shot?

John What tree shot?

Trevor The one where you lob the ball under the tree and I disappear into the branches. You won't find that shot in any text book ...

Spriggs exits silently into the garden

John Trevor, I've told you, I'll play under the tree in future. Not that it'll make any difference. You never win.

Trevor I won at school.

John That was a long time ago. Things were different then.

Trevor Yes, we had umpires.

John Trevor, I don't cheat. I don't need to. You're a loser: you always have been. You play under the tree because you don't expect to win, and that gives you an excuse to lose.

Trevor Does it?

John Trevor, why are we arguing like this? It's only a game.

Trevor Yes, but if you cheat at one thing, John, you'll cheat at another.

John Why? It's tennis — it's not life.

Trevor No, because in life you play on an unmarked court, the bounce is uneven, everyone cheats and there's no bloody umpire. That's life.

John (*staring*) I didn't know you felt like this. I thought you enjoyed our games. What brought this on. (*He stops*) My God! It was him again, wasn't it? What's the bastard doing to me? (*He looks around*) Where is he?
Trevor He's gone.
John Has he? (*He crosses to the hall door taking the gun from his pocket*) Well, he won't get far.
Trevor What are you going to do?
John I'm going to kill him ... Spriggs!

John crashes out of the door; simultaneously, Jenny enters with a towel

Jenny What's happening?
Trevor Spriggs has escaped. John's gone after him.
Jenny My God! He'll kill him.
Trevor That seems to be the general idea.

Jenny exits in pursuit

Trevor pours a drink

Barbara enters, glass in hand

Barbara Where's Spriggs?
Trevor He's gone.
Barbara You mean I've killed him?
Trevor No. The bullet's up there in the plaster. John's chasing him round the garden.
Barbara Aren't you going to help?
Trevor No.
Barbara (*curiously*) What's happened?
Trevor John and I had an argument.
Barbara What about?
Trevor Tennis.
Barbara (*disappointed*) Oh, is that all?
Trevor It went deeper than that.
Barbara How much deeper?
Trevor I called him a cheat. He called me a loser.
Barbara Well, where's the argument? I wouldn't quarrel with either of those statements.
Trevor What?
Barbara John doesn't mean to cheat. He just likes to win. He likes to win more than he likes to play. He'd be perfectly happy if you phoned your game in, just as long as he won. He's a winner, Trevor. That's why he won't partner me at doubles. He says I don't stand properly. He says I should

stand with my legs flexed, pantherish and ready to strike. I don't quite know what he means. He says I stand as if I'm waiting for a bus. Since I've never waited for a bus I don't know what that means either.

Trevor Is that what John really thinks of me: that I'm a loser?

Barbara It's difficult to know what John really thinks. He's a man of few words so one has to read a great deal from his expression which is unfortunate since his face is almost totally blank. I know he has mixed feelings about you.

Trevor Mixed feelings! I'm his oldest friend. We were at school together.

Barbara I know. (*Pause*) You bullied him, didn't you?

Trevor No, I protected him. I was head boy. I had to stamp out bullying.

Barbara Then why did you shut his hand in the desk and sit on the lid?

Trevor I didn't. Did he say that? You don't believe it, surely.

Barbara Well, it would explain those fat hands ...

Trevor I don't remember doing that.

Barbara You wouldn't — it wasn't your hand. And after all, it's what boys do, isn't it? We should be grateful it was just his hand.

Trevor He's never said anything to me about it. I don't remember any of this. He must have confused me with someone else.

Barbara You seem to have total amnesia where your school days are concerned, Trevor. Do you remember breaking his arm?

Trevor (*uneasily*) That was an accident. We were wrestling.

Barbara So you do remember that?

Trevor Yes.

Barbara You should do. He said it snapped like a twig. He spent all that summer with his arm in a plaster cast whilst yours was around Jenny's waist where his should have been.

Trevor Barbara, she doesn't even remember him from those days.

Barbara Not at all?

Trevor There was a crowd of us. She thinks she remembers a plaster cast sort of waving about in the background but that's all.

Barbara What a fickle thing memory is. He remembers her. He raves about her. Her blonde ponytail; her long brown legs. Mind you, he has seen a great deal of those legs just recently bending low over the net, pantherish and ready to strike and showing an abundance of frilly knickers.

Trevor I haven't noticed.

Barbara John has. It's affecting his service. His double faults have increased alarmingly.

Trevor (*after a pause*) Barbara, if John has these mixed feelings about me why does he ask me up here?

Barbara (*mischievously*) Can't you guess?

Trevor hesitates for a moment and then kisses Barbara

(*Staring at Trevor in surprise*) Why did you do that?

Trevor I felt like it.

Barbara Trevor, I've known you for years; you've never felt like it before. I always thought of you as a man who wouldn't take yes for an answer.

Trevor Are you saying yes?

Barbara (*moving away*) No.

Trevor Why not?

Barbara I'll let you into a little secret. I still love John but don't tell anyone.

Trevor I always thought it was the money.

Barbara No — that's just a delightful coincidence, Trevor.

Trevor Barbara .... (*He tries to move closer*)

Barbara (*moving away*) And I'll tell you something else that may surprise you. (*Pause*) I'm older than you are.

Trevor I know.

Barbara What?

Trevor Jenny said you were older.

Barbara Did she. (*She hesitates*) Suppose I said considerably older ... (*She studies him*) Suppose I said ... three years?

Trevor We thought about five.

Barbara Five! My God! I don't look it do I?

Trevor It doesn't matter, Barbara. (*He closes in on her*) You see, for some reason I've always preferred older women ...

Barbara It's probably because they can't run as fast.

Trevor I suppose it's all that knowledge — all that experience — all that history ...

Barbara Now I feel like a flight of steps worn by pilgrims. (*Pause*) Is it something to do with your mother?

Trevor Of course not. You're nothing like my mother.

Barbara Well, I'm certainly like someone's mother — probably John's. And he never looks any older. I long to see a fleck of grey or detect a limp, even hear a little creaking, but he seems to get younger. And now he's beginning to look at me broodingly. They say that's the first sign when your husband begins to look at you broodingly.

Trevor A sign of what?

Barbara That you're on the way out.

Trevor So is John the sort of man who can't take yes for an answer?

Barbara No, John's forgotten the question.

Trevor (*putting his arms around Barbara*) Well, I haven't ...

A pistol shot rings out

They start back from each other

Barbara That's John; he's shooting at Spriggs.

Two more shots

Trevor Sounds as if he's making sure of him.
Barbara One thing you can say about John — he's thorough.

Spriggs bursts in

Spriggs (*breathlessly*) Bugger this for a game of soldiers. Is there a church around here?
Trevor Why?
Spriggs I'm thinking of seeking sanctuary.
Barbara There's a church in the village but that's five miles away.
Spriggs I'll never make it. My blood pressure's sky-high. I'll probably have a heart attack.
Barbara It's your own fault; you will keep running about.
Spriggs Of course I keep running about! He's trying to kill me.
Barbara That's the trouble; you're bringing out his hunting instincts.
Spriggs In that case I'll stand perfectly still. He's too fond of that gun if you ask me. I think it's some sort of phallic symbol.
Barbara Well, things are improving; at least we have a symbol.

John enters followed by Jenny

Spriggs moves behind Barbara

John Come out from behind my wife.
Spriggs And get shot. No thanks. I'm safer here.
Barbara I wouldn't be too sure.
Jenny John, Spriggs isn't going to run away. Look at him — he's worn out.
Spriggs Look, I'll give you my word.
John Your word! One thing we've established this evening is that your word is frigging worthless.
Spriggs I couldn't escape even if I wanted to; I haven't got the strength.
John You aren't going to escape, Spriggs, because I'm going to lock you in the cellar.
Barbara Lock him in the cellar. Is that fair, John?
John What do you mean?
Barbara Aren't you forgetting the ... (*she whispers*) rats.
Spriggs What did she say?
John Nothing.
Barbara If he does have a weak heart.
John He hasn't got a weak heart.
Barbara But if he has.

John I'll leave the lights on.

Barbara That doesn't seem to make much difference. They're getting bolder.

Spriggs Christ! She did say rats. I'm not going down there. I can't stand rats.

Trevor I think we've found his weakness.

Spriggs My weakness! They're every bugger's weakness! I'm not going down there.

John You haven't any choice.

Spriggs Haven't I? (*He fishes the locket out of his pocket and dangles it in front of John*) Are you sure?

John (*hesitating*) Quite sure.

Trevor What's he got there?

Jenny My locket.

Spriggs I was going to return it. I hope it isn't damaged. I hope the hinge is all right. Perhaps you'd like to open it ...

Jenny It doesn't open.

Spriggs Oh, I thought it did. I thought it was the nature of a locket ... (*He dangles the locket in front of Jenny*)

Trevor moves unexpectedly and takes the locket from Spriggs and slips it into his pocket

Trevor I thought you were going to put him in the cellar?

John Yes. And you can stay there, Spriggs until you remember where they've taken my property.

Barbara Our property.

John (*coldly*) Our property. Get the cellar key, Barbara.

Spriggs But I can't stand rats.

John That's surprising; I should have thought you'd have been quite at home ...

John and Barbara exit with Spriggs

Trevor regards Jenny. He takes out the locket and turns it in his fingers. She holds her hand out but he doesn't give the locket to her

Trevor Well, at least we've got your locket back.

Jenny Yes.

Trevor Pity, though. We could have claimed for it. Money would have been useful.

Jenny It was my mother's.

Trevor Yes. I was forgetting.

Jenny (*after a pause*) We could still claim for it.

Trevor What?

Jenny Barbara says claim for everything. We pay enough insurance.

Trevor But you haven't lost it.

Jenny They don't know that. We could claim for some gold cuff-links as well.

Trevor I don't have any gold cuff-links.

Jenny You wouldn't if they'd been stolen.

Trevor I've never had any gold cuff-links.

Jenny They don't know that.

Trevor Stop saying that. It would be stealing, Jenny.

Jenny Does it matter?

Trevor Of course it matters.

Jenny Trevor, women are getting fifteen thousand pounds for having babies. I didn't.

Trevor What women?

Jenny Army women.

Trevor You weren't in the army.

Jenny A woman got twenty thousand pounds because they wouldn't let her be a motor mechanic.

Trevor You don't want to be a motor mechanic.

Jenny You can walk down the street, get bonked on the nose and end up with a thousand pounds.

Trevor You haven't been bonked on the nose.

Jenny I wish someone would bonk you on the nose.

Trevor What are you trying to say?

Jenny I want to know where we went wrong.

Trevor We didn't. But we will go wrong if we make a false claim. I'm surprised at you, Jenny.

Jenny Are you? Trevor, my washing machine is fifteen years old, likewise my fridge, and my oven door is secured by a leather strap. Have you seen their kitchen? And you say we haven't gone wrong.

Trevor Things will get better.

Jenny Will they?

Trevor We have to plan.

Jenny Plan! We've had three-year plans. We've had five-year plans. We've even had seven-year plans. We've had more plans than Soviet Russia. But things don't seem to get any better. You still creep into the wardrobe and count my shoes. You still switch the car engine off going down the hill, at grave risk to life and limb. And you even suggested that we open the bedroom curtains and undress by the light of the street lamp — until someone whistled from the street and shouted "Get 'em off".

Trevor It was only a suggestion. We have to make economies.

Jenny Well, I'm tired of making economies.

Trevor (*after a pause*) Is that what you want the money for — to do the kitchen?

Jenny No, I don't want to do the frigging kitchen.

Trevor Frigging?

Jenny I want to go to a beauty clinic. I want liposuction, and collagen, and I want to lighten my hair.

Trevor Why?

Jenny Because I always had more fun blonde.

She exits

Trevor opens the locket, studies it for a moment and then puts it away. He moves to the bookcase and opens it. He regards the safe for a moment

Trevor Two, five, one, nought, seven, six.

He turns the handle. The door fails to open. He looks relieved and smiles. He is about to turn away when the door swings open

Curtain

Scene 2

The drawing-room. Two hours later

The room is illuminated by a single table lamp. The safe is now closed and hidden by the bookcase

John reclines in an easy chair

Barbara enters. She crosses to the drinks tray. She turns, sees John and starts

John Why don't you get some sleep?

Barbara I'm not tired.

John Aren't you?

Barbara Do I look tired?

John I wouldn't know, would I?

Barbara What do you mean you wouldn't know? You'd know if I looked tired.

John Not any more. You could be looking your age ...

Barbara (*uneasily*) My age?

John (*after a pause*) Five years.

Barbara What?

John Five bloody years.

Barbara He told you.

John Yes. And he told me about the secret drawer in the escritoire. He knows more about you than I do. And he's only been here five minutes.

Barbara He finds other people's lives fascinating — he said so.

John Then he must certainly find yours fascinating. Is there anything else I should know? How many secrets have you got?

Barbara How many have you?

John (*after a pause*) Five years.

Barbara Don't keep saying that.

John No — six! You wouldn't even settle for being my age. You had to be a year younger. How's that for vanity.

Barbara Does it matter now?

John Of course it matters. It's false pretences.

Barbara False pretences. You mean like if you bought a car you'd expect the mileage to be correct?

John Yes.

Barbara I begin to feel more like an old Cortina every day.

John (*after a pause*) Five years.

Barbara Can't you think of it as five years' more maturity, more experience, more wisdom?

John No.

Barbara It's not important.

John If it's not important why did you lie about it, Barbara?

Barbara You may find this laughable but I was frightened of losing you.

John Or were you frightened of losing the money? That's why you married me, wasn't it? For the money.

Barbara You mean there was something else? I must have missed it.

John turns away

I didn't mean that, John.

John Don't worry, you won't hurt my feelings. I have a fairly low opinion of women.

Barbara No, John, you have a fairly low opinion of yourself. (*Brightly*) All right, there's five years between us but which five years?

John (*staring*) What do you mean which five years?

Barbara Well, if it was my first five years I did practically nothing but rest all the time. I was hardly out of my pram. It couldn't have been very ageing.

John You know which five years. The five years you've had that I haven't. The last five years.

Barbara But you were here the whole time.

John (*baffled*) You know what I mean. You're five years older. Five years more eating, breathing, walking ——

Barbara I never walk anywhere, you know that.

John What about up and down stairs? If you consider how many times you've climbed those in five years; it could add up to a week's walking.

Barbara I must say that does sound rather tiring.

John Not to mention what you did when you got there ...

Barbara What do you mean?

John I mean the bedroom. There must have been plenty of that during your lost five years.

Barbara Only in comparison with now. And you've nothing to complain about. I've given you everything a younger woman could, even children. And don't think it was easy keeping up with those young mothers who could give birth then run a mile. In fact, I've given you more. I've graced your table.

He laughs

Don't laugh. Before you met me you thought a side plate was somewhere to rest your elbow. You wanted polish, sophistication, and I gave it to you. I entertained your friends. I furthered your career. That's more than that black-bloomered nymph could have done.

John Black-bloomered nymph? What are you talking about?

Barbara (*picking up the statuette*) You know who I mean. God! I'd hit you with this only you'd accuse me of deliberately damaging it. You're such children. She doesn't even remember you. You're still pursuing those white ankle socks through the long grass and Trevor's probably got a thing about his infant teacher.

John Trevor?

Barbara He made a pass.

John What?

Barbara And do you know why? Because he felt entitled.

John Entitled? I don't know what you mean.

Barbara Don't you? And you talk about deceit.

John I'm talking about the fact that you lied to me. It was the act of an ageing bimbo.

Barbara Don't say that, John; don't say ageing. And as for "bimbo" I'm never sure what that means.

John A woman who bestows sexual favours for financial gain.

Barbara I thought that was a housewife.

John That's what you've always resented, isn't it? Being the wife. You've always been jealous of my success.

Barbara *Our* success.

John No — my success.

Barbara All right, John. You've been successful; you haven't discovered the secret of the universe.

John You know what you suffer from, don't you? Penis envy.

Barbara Penis envy! You mean yours? Describe it to me — I haven't seen it for some time. I seem to remember it wasn't much to look at.

John How dare you say that!

Barbara How dare you? I don't want a penis. I don't want to stand in a meadow shooting sparkling jets over the hedge, nor do I want to write my name in the snow, amusing as that might be. I want love, John.

John moves towards the garden door

Where are you going?

John Down to the Coopers again. They should be back by now. (*Gently*) Try and get some sleep.

He exits into the garden

Barbara crosses to pick up the bottle she drank from earlier. She hesitates, then leaves it

Barbara exits into the hall

Jenny puts her head around the double doors

Jenny (*whispering*) They've gone. Better come this way ... (*She comes into the room*)

Spriggs follows Jenny on. He is carrying an open bottle of wine. He looks around cautiously

Spriggs Where's Wyatt Earp?

Jenny (*looking out*) He's going down to the Coopers. Better give him a minute.

Spriggs Right. Want a drink?

Jenny No.

Spriggs It's a Mouton-Cadet '66. Very palatable. (*He drinks from the bottle*)

Jenny You shouldn't be doing that.

Spriggs I agree. I don't like drinking from the bottle. I'd prefer a little cut glass; it does enhance a drink. And a bit of cheese with it, possibly a rich Stilton. Mind you, that would have been virtual suicide down there. I'd have had the little buggers swarming all over me.

Jenny I mean you shouldn't be drinking his wine.

Spriggs I deserve it. It took me an hour to get the cork out. And if he didn't want me to drink his wine he shouldn't have locked me in the cellar.

Jenny (*moving to the garden window*) You'd better make your way across the fields. When you get to the lane you'll find it leads to a B-road ... What's the matter?

Spriggs Across the fields. That's going to play havoc with these suedes. And what about the cattle; I could hear them moving around out there ...

Jenny They're only cows; they won't hurt you.

Spriggs It would be just my luck to meet one with anthrax. Then there's the question of transport. I'm not going to get very far on foot.

Jenny What about the gang. Haven't you arranged a rendezvous?

Spriggs (*amused*) A rendezvous! That lot? They don't know the meaning of the word. They're rank amateurs. At the moment they're probably driving the wrong way down the M62 in a state of total panic. (*He sighs*) Softly will be in charge — now that's a receipt for disaster.

Jenny Softly?

Spriggs It's a bit of a misnomer really. Like some tall people are called Tiny. He's never done anything softly in his life. Like when we hit that Bond Street jewellers. Without a word to me he suddenly picks up a manhole cover and heaves it through the plate glass window. Everything starts ringing. And if that wasn't enough he then stands back to admire his handiwork and disappears straight down the manhole.

Jenny Look, I think you'd better go.

Spriggs Yes. Just one thing. (*Curiously*) Why are you doing this? And don't tell me it's because of the *Oxford Book of English Verse*, and it's not because of the locket. So why?

Jenny I don't like the idea of you going to prison.

Spriggs Why not?

Jenny You remind me of my father.

Spriggs Do I? Is he a crook?

Jenny (*shocked*) No — he's a magistrate.

Spriggs I can understand the confusion. Well, thank you for restoring an old man's faith in human nature. If it's any comfort to you this bottle of wine is the last thing I'll ever steal. If I do come back this way again it'll be for the maypole dancing. Now you'd better get back to your room before someone sees you.

Jenny Right. Good luck.

Spriggs And you.

Jenny creeps from the room

As Jenny leaves, Spriggs crosses to the garden door. He pauses, then takes a deep drink from the bottle and regards it for a moment

Well ... almost the last thing. (*He crosses to the bookcase and opens it*)

There is a sound of movement, off. Hearing this, Spriggs closes the bookcase and hides behind the curtains

Jenny enters stealthily. She looks thoughtfully at the anniversary cards for a moment and then crosses to the bookcase and opens it

Jenny (*softly*) Two, five, one, nought, seven, six ...

Spriggs' head appears around the curtains. There's a look of astonishment on his face

Jenny opens the safe

John enters from the garden

John What are you doing?
Jenny Oh. I thought I heard a sound. The safe was open.
John (*moving to the safe*) I can see that. Where's the money?
Jenny Someone's taken it.
John You're right. Someone has. (*He looks around*) Where have you put it?
Jenny Surely you don't think ——
John Well, since Spriggs is locked in the cellar you appear to be the prime suspect, Jenny.
Jenny How do we know he's in the cellar? Perhaps he's escaped. Stolen the money and made his way across the fields.

Another look of astonishment from Spriggs

John I don't think so. You worked it out, didn't you? I gave you a clue and you worked it out. That wasn't difficult for someone with ten frigging O levels. (*He shakes her*) I should have been more careful.
Jenny John, you're shaking me.
John I'll shake you like a salt cellar if you don't tell me where that money is.
Jenny I don't know.
John You were my ideal. I trusted you.
Jenny And you were my ideal.
John No, I wasn't. You didn't even remember me, you didn't even notice me. You always were a snob. The only reason you've changed is because of the money. Where is it?
Jenny You said you loved me.
John Yes, but not a hundred thousand pounds' worth. I was in love with the past. The smell of Pond's beauty cream, and grass, and young skin, and white ankle socks, and ponytails. (*He continues shaking her*) Where's that money?

Trevor enters

Trevor She hasn't got it.
John (*releasing Jenny and turning*) How do you know?
Trevor Because it wasn't there.
John What do you mean it wasn't there?
Trevor I looked and it wasn't there. Spriggs must have taken it.

Another shocked glance from Spriggs

John You don't expect me to believe that? I checked the money when I came
home. It was there. Spriggs hasn't had the opportunity.
Trevor Spriggs was alone in this room when I met him. He's taken it.
John No; you've taken it, the pair of you. You're in this together. You saw
your opportunity and you took it.
Trevor But we're your oldest friends. We were at school together.
John Yes, don't I remember. The girl with the turned-up nose and the head
boy, with his ten O levels and his six A levels — and where did it get you?
Pen pushing, shuffling papers and shining the seat of your pants. And I
remember the house with the double frontage, and your mother with the
faint odour of fish under her nose whenever she met me, and your frigging
father who treated me like a barrow boy. Well, none of it did you much
good, did it? Because it's not where you come from, Trevor, it's where
you're going.

Barbara enters

Barbara Oh. Am I interrupting something?
Jenny John's just accused us of taking his money.
Barbara Surely not. Trevor's your oldest friend and Jenny's the girl you ran
through the buttercups with. What's the world coming to?
John Barbara, if you haven't anything intelligent to say ——
Barbara But I have. I came to tell you that the cellar door's open and it looks
as if Spriggs has escaped.
John What?
Trevor What did I tell you? It was Spriggs.
John But how did he get away?
Trevor I don't know but he's obviously made a dash for it.
John Dash? He couldn't dash anywhere. He's totally out of condition.
You've heard him wheezing ... (*He sees the wine bottle*) Wait a minute.
How did this get here?(*He picks up the bottle*)

Spriggs' loud asthmatic breathing can be heard

(Listening) Sh! Listen, everyone.

They all listen

The loud asthmatic breathing continues, followed by the desperate sound of a spray

John takes the gun from his pocket and draws back the curtains

All right. Come out, Spriggs.

Spriggs emerges reluctantly

So it was you.
Spriggs Will you stop pointing that thing at me?
John Where's my money?
Spriggs I haven't got it.
John I'm going to count up to ten: if you don't tell me where it is ——
Barbara John, don't be silly.
John One ... two ... three ...
Spriggs My God! You'd do it wouldn't you? You just don't care. They say that if a criminal was confronted by the victims of his crime the effect would be salutary. Well, I've been confronted with my victims and the effect is more than salutary — it's bleeding frightening.
John Four ... five ... six ...
Barbara John.

Spriggs gets busy with his spray

John Seven ... eight .... nine ...
Spriggs I haven't got your money. Christ! Haven't you worked it out yet? Do you need the bleeding building to fall on you? Can't you see? She's got it. *(He points at Barbara)*
John What?
Spriggs She's just been waiting for the opportunity.
John My wife doesn't need the money. She's well-provided for.

Barbara gives John a sharp glance

Spriggs Is she? You're not thinking. Why was she so sure she hadn't set the alarm? Because she never sets the alarm. She wanted to be burgled.
John What do you mean?
Spriggs I mean she was prepared to gamble we wouldn't get into that safe,

even if we found it. But she could and all she had to do was wait. Blimey, she even left the back door open. We couldn't believe it.

John And neither can I. It wouldn't have worked. It didn't work.

Spriggs But it could have done. Remember your routine? You always garage the car while she switches off the alarm. That would give her plenty of time to empty the safe and blame the burglars. Unfortunately, she chose this particular night to get a little Brahms and Liszt ... so it took longer.

John You're lying, Spriggs: my wife doesn't even know the combination.

Spriggs (*staring*) Are you sure?

John Yes, you see, it's not just a question of trust. I'm saying she didn't have the opportunity.

Spriggs Couldn't she have found it out?

John Not Barbara — she hasn't that sort of mind.

Barbara (*quietly*) Two ... five ... one ... nought ... seven ... six ... Bingo.

John (*turning to Barbara in astonishment*) You knew?

Barbara Of course I knew. Although it took me a little time to work it out. I didn't realize you could be so sentimental.

John And you took the money?

Barbara Yes.

John But why? Haven't I always given you enough?

Barbara Yes — given. It's always given. Do you know what it's like asking you for money? I get sick to my stomach.

John You still ask.

Barbara It gets harder every year. You sign the cheque as if it's your death warrant.

John Well, it doesn't seem to stop you being extravagant.

Barbara On the contrary, I live quite frugally. If you'd bothered to look at me once in a while you'd see you've often paid for the same dress twice.

John What?

Barbara I pick the invoices up from the floors of dress shops.

John Why?

Barbara Because if I'm on the way out, John, I want to be well-provided for, as you quaintly put it.

John You would have been.

Barbara No, you'd have wriggled. You'd have fought. You'd have probably gone abroad. No-one gets your money easily — we've seen that tonight.

John (*bitterly*) Then you'll have to wait for me to die, Barbara.

Barbara I would but you're younger than I am. Besides, knowing you you'd probably take it with you. Like the old Viking Chief, your ship loaded with treasure, floating out into the North Sea with sails blazing. That's why I decided to start my fund.

John What fund?

Barbara For my old age, which according to you isn't far off. I call it — and this should amuse you — my "frig you" fund. Now, if you're not going to shoot me I'll go to bed. And don't keep me awake looking for the money because you won't find it.

John And you were prepared to let them take all our things just to get the money?

Barbara Your things, John. (*She moves to the hall door*)

John When are you leaving?

Barbara (*turning*) Leaving? I'm not leaving: why should I?

John Then why?

Barbara Why? Because now I can leave if I want to. (*She kisses him lightly on the lips*) So watch out.

Barbara exits

Trevor and Jenny — particularly Jenny — glare reproachfully at John

John slowly becomes aware of this

John Jenny, I'm sorry: what can I say?

Jenny Nothing. Trevor, I'm going to pack.

John Jenny ——

Jenny By the way, I did remember you, John. Vividly. Your trousers were always ridiculously short and you smelled of fish and chips ...

Jenny exits

John catches Trevor's eye

John Trevor ... I'm sorry — I ...

Trevor That's all right.

John I don't know what came over me. How did it happen ...?

Spriggs Well, I think I'll be making tracks now ...

John Where did it all go wrong? Everything's spoilt ... (*His brooding gaze falls on Spriggs*)

Spriggs (*uneasily*) I think I'd better be off. I wouldn't worry about it; these things are better out in the open ... and they always look different in the morning ...

John It's you, isn't it? Ever since you came things have gone wrong.

Spriggs (*backing away*) No.

John (*advancing*) Yes, they have. You've never stopped prying and probing, turning us inside out, interfering in our lives, tainting our relationships. You haven't just stolen my things, you've stolen my life, you bastard. (*He pushes the pistol hard against Sprigg's chest*)

Trevor Don't, John!

John pulls the trigger; the gun gives a loud click

Spriggs gasps

John (*after a pause*) It's all right. I left the catch on.

Spriggs stares down dumbly at his chest, then falls back. He sprays into his mouth urgently, chokes and tries to loosen his tie. He staggers this way and that about the room, John and Trevor standing by helplessly, making ineffective attempts to catch him. He is offered a glass of water which is sent crashing to the ground. He produces a bottle of tablets but they are scattered on the carpet. He manages to cram a few into his mouth then coughs and spits them out again. He finally falls with a heavy thud. Trevor bends over him for a moment

Trevor That's torn it.
John What?
Trevor He's dead.
John Are you sure?
Trevor Well, he's stopped breathing — that's usually a sign. He's dead all right.
John And I've caused it. What have I done, Trevor?
Trevor (*firmly*) Nothing. There are no witnesses. He simply had a heart attack. Let me get rid of that gun. (*He takes the gun from John*)
John Poor little devil. You know. I don't feel any bitterness towards him now.
Trevor (*crossing to the window*) I'm sure he'll appreciate that. John — the lights are on at the Coopers.
John What?
Trevor You'd better get down there and ask them to dial 999.
John Yes, of course. (*He moves to the door and pauses*) And thanks, Trevor. (*He looks down at Spriggs*) You know, he really was in the wrong line of work ...

John exits

Trevor (*after a pause*) You can get up now.
Spriggs I can't — I'm dead.
Trevor You're not dead.
Spriggs I am while he's around. What did I tell you: he's a raving psychopath. I was in Pentonville with a bloke like him; used to eat razor blades with his cornflakes.

Trevor Then you'd better go before he comes back.

Spriggs (*getting to his feet*) What will you tell him?

Trevor I'll tell him you made an unexpected recovery. God! I'm not a doctor.

Spriggs Right. Well, I hope you won't think too harshly of me when I'm gone.

Trevor (*staring*) Too harshly?

Spriggs I mean, there was nothing personal in this.

Trevor Nothing personal. Spriggs, it was entirely personal. John was right. We haven't been burgled, we've been personally violated.

Spriggs And what about me? I was looking for guidance, high principles and leadership. And what do I find? Moral laxity and spiritual decay. It's been very disappointing.

Trevor What?

Spriggs Don't blame this one on me; blame it on society. It's sick.

Trevor I'm not blaming this on society, Spriggs. You're an old rogue and always have been. And society would be well rid of you.

Spriggs Then why are you letting me go?

Trevor Because I think it would be safer for all concerned.

Spriggs Or is it because you opened that safe? Tell me something; if the money had been there would you have taken it?

Trevor (*after a pause*) I don't know.

Spriggs No, none of us do until we're tested, Trevor. What you had there was the first insidious whiff of corruption. It's like your first cigarette — you know it's not going to do you any good but you can't resist it. Now, how do I get to the A17?

Trevor Well, you go in a northerly direction until you get to Clumber Farm then you turn due west ——

Spriggs (*sighing*) Northerly direction — due west. What happened to right and left and straight ahead? God! I hate the country. I'll need a car to meet me. Mind if I use the phone? I have to ring the Queens Hotel, Leeds.

Trevor You've cut the wires.

Spriggs I know. Now, where did I put it ...?

Spriggs lifts a plant out of its pot and recovers a cellular phone

Trevor You mean it was there all the time?

Spriggs Yes. (*He dials*) I'll leave something for the call. (*Into the phone*) Hallo? Queens Hotel? Could you put me through to Mrs Beaudine, please.... Yes. I know it's late but it is urgent. ... What? Not listed? Ah. Well, would you put me through to Mrs Patterson?... Yes. Patterson. ... She's not? Oh.... No, I'm not trying to waste your time. Look, do you have a Mrs Travis-Kemp registered there? ... You do. Good. Would you put me through please: I'm her husband. Thank you. (*Lowering his voice*) Hallo.

Tango one here. Listen carefully. I know it's late but I want you to get the car out and ... What do you mean, you can't? Listen — I'm stuck out here in the bleeding wilds. I'm surrounded by anthrax, fowl pest and foot and mouth disease. I'm also being pursued by green wellies with guns. I want you here now — if not sooner. ... Why not? ... What? ... What? I don't believe it.

Trevor What's happened?

Spriggs The car's been stolen — from a secure car park —- in broad daylight. What's this country coming to?

Trevor begins to laugh

What are you laughing at?

CURTAIN

FURNITURE AND PROPERTY LIST

ACT I

SCENE 1

On stage: Bookcases. *On them*: Leatherbound books including *Encyclopaedia Britannica*. *Behind them*: safe with pistol inside
On mantelpiece: key
Easy chairs
Sofa
Sideboard. *In it*: glasses
Table. *On it*: drinks
Table lamp
Pot plants. *In one pot*: cellular phone
Contents of sideboard drawers
On shelves: anniversary cards, white alabaster statuette
Telephone

Off stage: Golf club (**Trevor**)

Personal: **Spriggs:** pocket folder, asthma spray (used throughout), bag of wrapped sweets

SCENE 2

Off stage: Statuette (**Jenny**)
Tumbler (**Barbara**)
Pistol (**John**)
Rope (**Trevor**)

Personal: **Spriggs**: butterfly brooch

ACT II

SCENE 1

Off stage: Cigarette, lighter (**Jenny**)
Towel (**Jenny**)
Glass (**Barbara**)

Personal: **Spriggs**: locket

SCENE 2

Re-set: Safe and bookcase closed

Off stage: Open bottle of wine (**Spriggs**)

Personal: **John**: pistol
             Spriggs: bottle of wine

LIGHTING PLOT

Practical fittings required: table lamp
One interior. The same throughout

ACT I, SCENE 1

To open: General interior lighting

No cues

ACT I, SCENE 2

To open: General interior lighting

No cues

ACT II, SCENE 1

To open: General interior lighting

No cues

ACT II, SCENE 2

To open: Single table lamp with covering lighting

No cues